THE ULTIMATE STRESS-FREE PRODUCTIVITY SECRETS

THE ULTIMATE STRESS-FREE PRODUCTIVITY SECRETS

GET BETTER IN BUSINESS, LIFE AND RELATIONSHIPS

MANIKANTA BELDE

Notion Press

Old No. 38, New No. 6
McNichols Road, Chetpet
Chennai - 600 031

First Published by Notion Press 2016
Copyright © Manikanta Belde 2016
All Rights Reserved.

ISBN 978-1-946390-61-5

This book has been published with all efforts taken to make the material error-free after the consent of the author. However, the author and the publisher do not assume and hereby disclaim any liability to any party for any loss, damage, or disruption caused by errors or omissions, whether such errors or omissions result from negligence, accident, or any other cause.

No part of this book may be used, reproduced in any manner whatsoever without written permission from the author, except in the case of brief quotations embodied in critical articles and reviews.

CONTENTS

Acknowledgement: ix
Praise For xi
About the Author xiii
About the Book xv
Wait a Moment… xvii
Introduction xix

PART ZERO

The Difference, you Should Know 3
Develop Just-Do-it and Do-it-now approach 6
Get Inspired 8

PART ONE

1. The Old Golden Rule Still Works 13
2. How to Deal with Interruptions and Distractions? 17
3. Mental Energy is Directly Proportional to Relaxation Time 23
4. Develop "Why?" 27
5. Develop Habits That Control Your Will Power 30
6. Believe It - Time of Your Death Is Fixed 33
7. Just Do it Strategy 36
8. Moment of Inspiration is an Illusion Unless You Start Pursuing An Action 39
9. Use Limited Time and Unlimited Energy 41
10. How to Gain Self-Control? 44
11. How to Complete any Task Faster? 49
12. How Every Small Task Counts? 52
13. Smart Cuts Will Help You Perform Better 55

14. Stay Action-Oriented	58
15. Crafting Effective Plan	61
16. Get Balanced Mind	65
17. Practice "Best Thinking Habits."	68
18. Improve Every Day and Evaluate	76

PART TWO

19. Reconstructing or Build New Pathways of Processes	83
20. Developing Accuracy and Speed	86
21. Transform Travel Time to Productive Time	90
22. Organize Workspace	92
23. Creating Action Posters	97
24. Plan 'it' in advance	100
25. Act Like an Introvert	103
26. Try 50/50 Rule	106
27. Use Filtering Method	108
28. Curing Procrastination	110
29. Stop worrying about results	113
30. Recharging helps you become productive	116
31. Do Not Rush to Accomplish	118
32. Now and Later Charts Help you Become Better	120
33. Work Alone is not Important	124
34. Creative Works Versus Formal Works	129
35. Convert Morning Time to Productive Time	131

PART THREE

36. Take This Weapon Wherever you go	137
37. Small Lists Work Better	139
38. Rapport Methods for Transformation	141
39. CCMU Method Works Great	144

40. How to Stop Over Thinking?	146
41. How to Prevent Fear And Kill Doubts?	148
42. Minimizing Addictions	152
43. Follow this Golden Principle	154
44. Working Repeatedly is not Right	156
45. Creating Vision Chart	158
46. Feel free but Be-costlier	161
47. Share it for Free Reminders	164
48. Change 'E' Frequently	166
49. Avoid unnecessary Talks and Meetings	168
50. Bait Works, Use It	170

PART FOUR

Inspiration Time	175
More Things to Know	177
Signing Off Message	179

PART FIVE

Summary	183
Productivity Quotes you Could use in Your Life	193

PART SIX

Assessment Resources	199

PART SEVEN

Other Works by Author	203

Acknowledgement:

My heartfelt thanks

To my family and friends who always believed, encouraged and helped me always. Without whom I wouldn't accomplish this great work on time without fail.

Thanks to everyone

Who supported and worked for me to accomplish this task very successfully.

Praise For

The Ultimate Stress-Free Productivity Secrets

It's really inspiring and helpful for you who wish to be productive and fruitful. I suggest it's a must read book.

—**Sathya**, Life coach and consultant.

Manikanta Belde has addressed the daunting task of personally experimenting with any and every technique you can envision that could positively affect your productivity life. His dedication to the project and his perceptive conclusions combined with his honesty and articulateness, make this an interesting and useful guide.

—**Narayana**, Entrepreneur.

The author talks and suggests very practical solutions about how to solve and make your productivity life at next level during the real tight schedule of the day. Feel very free from floating of ideas.

—**Ram**, Freelancer.

This is a book that promises, in the title, to pay for itself and, the truth is, it will, in just a few days. And you will even enjoy the reading journey. I suggest everyone read this book.

—**Swetha**, Social media expert.

This book is a must for anyone wanting productivity life while enjoying and accomplishing the things they are passionate about in life. I actually read the whole book in one night, and my only regret is that I didn't discover this guide sooner.

—**Tarun**, Microbiologist.

This book is really inspiring and teaches you real effective methods to transform your normal life into productive life which is interesting and worth living. Thanks for the knowledge shared.

—**Aneesh**, H.R.

A must read guide who is really interested in getting more out of less and who really want to control and accomplish things in time and have a successful life.

—**Rohit,** Engineer.

It's really a fantastic guide which is worth reading. It really helps you change your life to productive life without fail if you use the techniques carefully.

– **Sai**, Student.

About the Author

Manikanta Belde is an autodidact who is interested in several subjects. He completed his Graduation. He is doing his Masters in Business Administration. He is an author of few fiction and non-fiction series books. His works are widely accessible and inspiring. He is the author of top writings- Quotes of Wisdom, The Rhythm of Life, The Last Tree of Wishes and Surprising Science Behind Indian Superstitions.

He began his writing journey when he is 18 years old with inspiring lines which are collectively called as "Quotes of Wisdom" which are still on top section on the web and received the first appraisal from the people. He then soon started writing short stories, novels, self-help guides and research guides.

He is a creative and innovative public speaker who gave several talks to students on creative learning, innovation, entrepreneurship, time management, etc. His passion for sharing knowledge and wisdom made him contribute significant resources which transform or enhance the life of people. His works are sagacious, innovative and helpful in all the possible ways.

He is also an entrepreneur who founded MMW, seasonal hub, Zero Web tech, and Bla-Bla computer solutions, etc. He also provided his services to several charity centers therefore considered as a philanthropist.

He is a visionary who believes that "real passionate visions and actions can transform this world into a beautiful heaven when efforts are put into work." He also believes that "burning desires in you, pave the path to great success in life."

He is also a consultant who is expert in areas such as business development, relationships, time management and innovative learning. He guided and helped people make their conditions better with his methods and ideas.

About the Book

The ultimate stress-free productivity secrets, is a guide that guides through next level productivity strategies which will enhance your time management abilities. It also transforms your regular life into exciting life which is full of hopes, success, and good relations. This source helps people become more attentive to how they spend time and also teaches them how to manage time properly.

This book is designed in a way that all methods are quoted in a particular order that makes it easier for readers to read and follow every process that has been shared in this book.

This book isn't just a guide which will guide you through techniques that make you productive but also it's a resource that inspires you to live productive life every day with high energy. This guide also transforms your attitude towards your unsatisfied life into the approach that brings you satisfaction and success at the same time.

The words in this book are well written and ordered in a particular manner that will help you get most out of this guide and helps you become better in your business, life, and relationships. The only thing you should do is believe in you first and then have little of your belief in this guide that it will transform your life by making you productive.

This book is not limited to a particular group of people, but this is a useful guide who wants a change in their life. This book is written to meet everyone needs to become productive and succeed at every step of their life. This book is for everyone including artists, business guys, authors, teachers, professors, students, doctors, lawyers, etc…, who has the real zeal to transform their world into the best place they have ever lived before.

Believe that you can change anything in life and with such belief comes the ways that help you transform your lives and get success, satisfaction, and peace. Your belief can help you get rid of habits which drag you down in life.

Learn all the methods and techniques from this book carefully. Read again and again till you know how you can apply these principles in your practical life.

Wait a Moment...

A few facts you should know

Multitasking decreases productivity levels and increases stress levels.

Only 22% of the time in a day is used and remaining 78% is wasted for nothing.

Stressful mind results in unproductive life.

People who have more than 7.5 hours of sleep and less than 9 hours of sleep seem to become productive than others.

Happier people are more productive.

By taking 1 hour per day for independent study, 7 hours per week, 365 hours in a year, one can learn at the rate of a full-time student. In 3-5 years, the average person can become an expert on the topic of their choice, by spending only one hour per day.

It takes approximately 30 days to learn a new habit.

These are some facts you should know but don't believe and limit your mind accepting these facts as true because they are in ordinary circumstances which mean they are not true always. Never accept anything easily if you don't find proofs. Do not understand without experiencing.

Many people get attracted to facts, and this attraction makes them believe every fact as truth which is not fair. Therefore don't get tempted for attractive headlines or points. There are several resources written in an interesting way, but they don't help when you move forward reading them. Therefore never judge anything soon. Always take the time to understand and be patient while learning anything.

Introduction

Do you want to be a productive person?

Do you want to be a productive person quickly?

Do you want to have more control over time in your life?

Do you want to make your life interesting and worth living?

Do you want to get better in life, business and relationships?

Then you are at right place. This guide would be for you if you answered yes to all the questions. This guide will help you get answers to the questions above.

This book is a guide that will transform your life. This book is naturally written in a way that it is easy to understand and all the methods and hacks published in the book can be readily applicable, and they are profoundly transforming and inspiring ways. Learn every way in this book by heart and make use of every method very carefully.

This guide gives most of the people "ability to change." This is an effective guide for people who really want to transform their life into productive one. This also helps you teach others how to become more productive applying the methods presented in this resource. So learn and utilize every method correctly to get desired results.

Although human has natural ability to be active and productive in his life, the modern world lifestyle made him loose his natural ability and made him confused and sometimes lazy. With a little discipline, anyone can become more productive and will be able to find success, peace, and satisfaction in life.

You can use the extra time you saved, to fulfill your passion and dreams. You could bring your visions and ideas come true into reality which gives you more success and satisfaction. You will learn to gain and save extra time. You will also get to use this time to become more productive by doing what you love.

Every method in this guide, when used correctly, optimizes your productive life. You will learn to live extra productive life with enthusiasm and high energy.

This book mostly uses simple language that everyone can understand easily. I believe that the most important thing is to deliver the knowledge properly rather that making a book or writing look so sophisticated that not everyone can understand.

This book is for you. This book will change your living way when methods in this book are used correctly. I have written this book to share all possible ways which help you build your day correctly and enhances your living conditions.

Call it the dark time spending life doing nothing. Many people face dark time at some point in their life. I have met several people and listened to their ideas and dreams which were great but in action they were illusions. People always complain that they have no time to fulfill their dreams or wishes. Few people complain that they lose interest in things they have started and so they quit soon without reaching their destiny. The reasons for their failures are endless. Everybody have their own reason of excuse to share. I found that most people have few things in common which fail them succeed all the time. The things include lack of time, loss of interest, fear of failure, too many doubts, and over thinking, etc.

Above things are common barriers for most of the people in this modern world. Our busy lives have made us think less and work more. We are living in illusions and with confusion minds most of the time. There should be some solution to end all these problems and live a peaceful, healthy, productive and fruitful life.

That is why I have written this guide to show people the path to real successful living. Few people may feel it is tough to change but believe me when you believe in "change," everything is possible in this world. Believe in you and believe in change and then results, you expected will pour in automatically. Let me tell you why I have decided to write this book. There is a strong reason to share this knowledge with you.

It was in 2014. I am doing my graduation, and I have seen people working so hard at that time, and also I have seen individuals who are doing smart work. I have also seen individuals who are not working at all and people call them the lazy. Inspired from around situations I want to change the people around me to work efficiently by enhancing their thinking and encouraging them to live this short and sweet life in a productive way.

Let me tell you the story of these two guys. For convenience let's name them Mr. X and Mr. Y. Mr. X is hard working, sincere guy who really has a strong ability to work for a longer time. He is the busy guy who always sticks to some work. He has no time for enjoyment or celebrations.

Mr. Y is smart working, passionate guy who really has high mental ability and confidence and he works for very less time than expected, and he is not a busy guy but productive. He spends his saved time on his dream projects as well as he spends his time with his family. Both guys complete projects provided to them. But the thing is Mr. X starts early and ends on time, and Mr. Y starts late and finishes on or before the deadline given. Even though, Mr. X works so hard he could not succeed as much as Mr. Y has reached.

This is a true story from which I have realized that being busy or hard working doesn't give you success but being productive do. These two guys story made me discover the difference between being busy and being productive. I found that only a few people who are really successful are the productive people and they are not busy guys. Several people are busy, and hard working who earning money is, and if they have no satisfaction, then they are not considered as successful at all.

I have seen most people like Mr. X and felt pity, and so I have brainstormed and researched for all the methods that would convert the life of individuals like Mr. X into Mr. Y. So to make this world full of people who have peace, satisfaction, and success I have written this guide which I hope will show you the path to life transformation.

I told you that you will get better in business, life and relationships by using this guide. It's all possible by using time efficiently. Time is what you can't buy, how much rich you may be? So managing your time effectively and using it on vital things in life will ultimately get you better in business, life, and relationships.

I encourage you to learn and use all tools, rules, and methods very carefully by applying them practically in your life and see the results. As the subtitle states "get better in life business, life, and relationships," you will get the proof for the statement through the results you will obtain after utilizing this guide actually. Thank you for having this guide, and I wish you all the best for creating a productive life which is worth living, pleasing and satisfactory.

Seven things this book will help you achieve

Become a better person at relationships, life, and business.

It gives you the ability to transform your present living conditions.

Complete any task or project in or on time without fail.

Increase your efficiency at work.

It helps you build stronger influence on people around you and your work.

It helps you live an extra stress-free day in your life.

Teaches you to learn new skills easily and efficiently and helps you save more time on every task you have to accomplish.

This book will answer these questions

How you can transform your leisure time into productive time?

How to accomplish tasks in time without fail?

How to enhance or develop your skills so fast?

What is the difference between busy and productive people?

How to stop procrastination?

How to be successful in planning and executing?

What works best for you?

How to transform your lazy life?

How to get out of the box and think wise?

How to create a best time management plan for a day?

Nine suggestions on how to get most out of this book

1. Don't give a glance, read every method clearly and think of getting most out of it by applying it to yourself in the way that suits you. You should have a sincere desire to learn which is prerequisite to get most out of this book.
2. Topic headlines may tempt you but don't rush into things. Read every topic carefully but analyzing each and every strategy.
3. Stop frequently in your reading to think about what you are reading. Ask yourself how and when you can apply each method.

4. Read with crayon, pencil, pen, magic marker or highlighter in your hand. I suggest you take a paper or notebook and note down important things and also use them to construct paths that are applicable for your life transformation.
5. Don't just skim at once. After reading the book thoroughly read it at least once a month to get real benefits of reading this guide.
6. Don't just read the book because a human doesn't learn just by reading but they learn by doing and practicing again and again.
7. Record and analyze progress at every step you make use of these strategies. Maintain a development book and see which method works best for you.
8. Keep notes to track back of this book showing how and when you have applied these methods.
9. Develop a great enthusiasm and interest while reading the book and believe in "you" at every step and believe in "change."

PART ZERO

The Difference, you Should Know

The difference you should be aware deals with Being busy and being productive. It helps you understand the differences between busy and productive people. There are two kinds of people when comes to time management. They are busy people and productive people. Many people think both as same. But when we peek into depths, it can be seen that both are completely different and in fact both seem to be opposite to each other.

Before moving on let me tell you the differences between Busy and Productive people. These differences give you a clear idea of which group you are in and this you help you transform your ways and living, based on your self-judgment.

Busy people traits:

They always work hard and get no desired results.

They have no time to spend with the family.

They have no peace and satisfaction.

They think fast and make wrong judgments.

They always boast that they are busy.

They have ill health because of working for a long time.

They have several goals to accomplish.

They have no time for other things.

They have no proper mission.

These people have many priorities at a time.

They quickly act without thinking well.

They have more distractions or interruptions because they open all the doors of their mind.

They multitask without focusing.

They make plans that fail mostly.

They are always doing something to be busy.

They pleasantly pass their time in different, unusual activities.

They are process oriented.

They lose focus very soon.

They exhaust their energy on less important tasks.

They don't know "why?" they do.

They are not open to change and innovation.

They work for money.

They always feel something is missing in their life even though they work hard.

They live in illusions and confusion most of the time.

Productive people traits:

They work hard and get desired results.

They spend time with their family.

They have peace and satisfaction in life.

They think clearly and make right judgments.

Their work speaks more than they talk.

They have better health and success.

They have priorities to work on.

They spend time wisely on important things.

They have a proper mission.

They have few priorities at the time.

They think clearly, and then they act.

They have less or no distractions or interruptions because they close all the doors of their mind and work with full concentration to accomplish their goals.

They focus clearly on important tasks.

They create perfect plans that always bring success.

They are always doing something meaningful.

They focus their energy on what is important.

They are result oriented.

They can focus on things for a longer time.

They make practical use of their energy on important tasks.

They know "why?" accurately.

They work for a cause.

They always feel that they have to accomplish one greater thing after every success.

They always had a strong belief in change and innovation.

They live in reality and makes right decisions at the right time with clear thinking.

Analyzing these traits, you can judge yourself into one of the categories and then you can change the ways you are moving in and find innovative ways to live better every day. This list also helps you analyze other people and make proper judgments and then assist them to overcome their time management problems. This guide is not just to change you but also to alter the people around you and help them, find peace and success.

These are the most important differences you should know before you judge yourself or others regarding busy and productive. Reading and understanding the above statements clearly gives you the difference between two kinds of people. Let's go on further to explore the best knowledge in this guide.

DEVELOP JUST-DO-IT AND DO-IT-NOW APPROACH

Before getting most out of this guide, you have to develop a just-do-it approach in you. This helps you learn faster and use most methods in this guide work for you. What is this method? How does it work? How to develop it? All these questions are answered in this part. This section will help you develop a just-do-it approach and helps you focus more on actions rather than words.

This approach states that, just-do-it & do-it-now. It always tries to teach you to do things quickly without procrastination. It's a simple formula which has a greater impact. It will help you save your time and use the time you saved on your other passion projects or dreams.

It works great when you practice this approach and get expertise in using this simple method. It helps you become action oriented. It will help you talk less and work more efficiently. This process makes you accomplish tasks faster and lets your accomplished tasks speak about you.

I am going to teach you the method to develop "just do it approach mindset," it's really easy to learn and very simple method when used correctly with a whole heart and stable mind.

This method comprises of three components. They are Environment, Situation, and mind. Knowing how to control these three elements will help you develop this approach to you quickly. These three elements are major influences which make this method work or fail.

Influencers of Just-Do-It approach- Environment, Situation, and Mindset

Environment:

People behavior and belief system are built on base on the environment they live in. So environment has a significant influence on everyone. But don't act according to environment every time. This won't help you succeed. You have to build right beliefs irrespective of what environment you had lived in or living in. The wisest always maintain control over views without allowing the environment to affect them. They are same everywhere. They know accurately what is right and what is wrong. They build their behavior and beliefs based on only logical analysis and proofs.

Situation:

The situation is where we act in a particular way. We all act according to situations but not against situations. So you have to bring control over a situation after proper thinking and making right decisions. Gaining control over the situation makes it easy to develop "I can do" mindset. I can do mindset builds greater confidence and strong belief in accomplishing anything.

Mindset:

Having right mindset is imperative. Without it, you can't change anything. You should have a stable mindset with great confidence and belief in you. Mindset is built based on your beliefs. Therefore environment has its influence on building right mindset in an indirect way.

When you can bring these three components in your control, it becomes easy for you to achieve what you want in time. It becomes easy to become a "doer," it helps you build "just do it and do it now approach" mindset. You will get refrained from over thinking which mostly leads to failures and sorrows by use of this method.

Get Inspired

I know building a mindset is comfortable than establishing the same mindset for a longer time. So to create a mindset that is stable for a longer time, I encourage you to get inspired. Get inspired by doing or accomplishing tasks you love. Do something paramount to become more inspired and maintain a great mindset.

This is the story of my good old friend. He always rushes in doing things, and he always wants to complete tasks in or before the deadlines, and he always does. He shows interest and enthusiasm in accomplishing tasks he has been given to do, even though he hates the work few times. He speaks very less and works so much in an efficient manner.

One day I asked him why he rushes in accomplishing any task so fast. He answered smiling that he has limited time but not limited energy. I said what? He replied that he wished to tell me a story of one of his friend. So I said okay go on.

He started the narrating story of his friend. He stated that he had a friend who is really ambitious to get success and he added that his friend used to share some great dreams and desires he wished to fulfill in life. Then he said that his friend used to say he will accomplish them soon but he never took any initiative to achieve his dreams because of fear of failure and some other reasons.

The time passed by, and he said that his friend never tried to fulfill his dreams. He never took any action to fulfill his dreams and desires and one day all of a sudden news came saying that his friend was dead caused due to some ill health problem. He stated that he was surprised to hear news of his friend's death and he stated that he started quivering and he didn't know what's happening in his mind at that time. He became idle for a while in shock.

He remembered what his friend spoke to him several times, and he remembered his dreams and desires shared with him. But he is no more that day, and he said that his friend accomplished nothing. He said that this situation had shown a larger impact on him.

He felt sorry for his friend's loss, and after few days he decided to accomplish any goals, tasks or dreams as soon as possible because no one knows what's our deadline. He exaggerated that being dead without any satisfaction doesn't seem to be right for him. That's why he started to speak and relax less and works more to accomplish his desires and dreams.

He also talked that we all have one beautiful, short and sweet life to live and so we should never over think because over thinking leads to doubts and fear that kill our dreams which I have experienced all the time. So I decided to limit my thinking process before it becomes over thinking.

He felt like words won't change anything, but actions do it more efficient way. So he decided to keep it as the principle of his life. Speak less and work more efficiently and the results obtained from your job will surely show what you are to the world.

After listening to my friend's story, I felt that it's true that you have limited time and unlimited energy which you can use to accomplish any dream or goal that bring you satisfaction. There are things we can't buy and time is one among them so use it very carefully before you end up knowing its importance after you lose it.

PART ONE

1. The Old Golden Rule Still Works

"Health is wealth. Acquired wealth could be used to stay healthy."

This old golden rule is very popular which is known to everyone. It is hoary, but it works even now. The rule is very simple-"Health is Wealth."

Yeah, it's that's simple. What do you think more than that? But the law doesn't work as simple as it seems to be. Most people know this rule, but they never worry about it. I know even most of you who are reading this book knows this rule, but you may think what's the connection between health and productivity. But let me abridge the golden rule which will help you build a relationship.

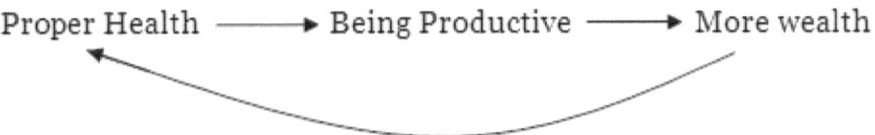

Did you find the link? Yeah, you are right, productivity is a middle step of health and wealth. Being healthy doesn't make you wealthy but being healthy and performing productive tasks will produce wealth. This is the real cycle you have to understand which inspire you to stay healthy which results in productive life and this will in turn results in wealthy living. These three components in the cycle depend on each other to maintain stability.

We know a machine runs efficiently if we manage it properly by providing everything it needs to stay in good condition. The same way our human body works. The Even human body needs maintenance as a machine does. Our human body should be provided with healthy food, proper sleep, and several other things to stay fit.

So before, becoming productive, become healthier and then productivity and wealth can be obtained through your efforts.

Some of the researchers stated the following results which show the relation between healthy lifestyle and productivity.

1. Employees who take healthy food were more likely to have 30-40% higher job performance.
2. Employees who ate fruits and vegetables at least 3 to 4 time a week were 20% more likely to be productive.
3. our brain to work at its best requires a constant supply of glucose and fat.
4. taking high energy producing food helps people focus and work for a longer time.

You have learned the importance of healthy food for productivity. So now find all the foods that help you become productive. There are several resources you can find about foods that help you become productive. Go through every resource very carefully and make a right diet plan that works best for you.

One fine day a man met me and spoke that he has all wealth he needs but no peace or good health and he went on talking about his living conditions. He mainly worried about his health and he said that no amount of money is able to cure his health conditions correctly. He also stated that he had worked intensively to gain wealth without taking care of his health which is now not at all easy to cure and he also added that he is unable to do anything properly because he was unable to focus on any work precisely due to his ill health.

What he said is true. No amount of wealth can make your disease get cured; no amount of money can bring you peace. It's our duty to take care of health along with being productive. If you have good health, you can have anything which includes wealth and peace in life. If you have adverse health conditions, and also you have unlimited money, this doesn't make any difference. Without proper health, nothing is so important in your life as your bad health makes you suffer rather than you enjoy your living which is why health is crucial.

The monk named Dalai Lama when asked by a man this question "what is really surprising about humanity?"

Then the monk answered that "Man sacrifices his health to make a lot of money in his life and the same man sacrifices his wealth to recuperate his health.

Always Keep this in mind, how you maintain your health has a direct impact on your productivity life.

These Productivity tips help you focus more and accomplish work faster.

1. Early to bed and early to rise

Go to sleep at the right time and get up early and this will help you have enough sleep which is imperative for becoming healthy and productive. The important thing is you have to sleep for enough time. Going early to bed and getting up early in the morning helps your brain work actively and several types of research have proved it. The early morning time is vital time for performing necessary tasks. Therefore it is crucial to get up early and start working on meaningful projects. During morning hours you have fewer distractions and peaceful mind. Therefore, it helps you focus more on any work you do at this time. You will find more about the importance of morning hours in future chapters of this book.

Early morning workouts will enhance mind abilities by stimulation of endomorphins in the brain which will give a boost to your brain, and many wealthy people who are passionate about their life follows this rule because they know the importance or morning time.

2. Eat right food at the right time.

It is important to eat the right food at the right time. You must eat when you feel hungry, and this is crucial to overcoming any internal or digestion problems which may up come in the future. Eating right or proper food is also imperative. Your body gets constructed based on what you eat. Eat foods that make you active and healthier. Avoid junk food mostly because it has a lot of effects on your health. Eat the right amount of food, and this is also vital to maintain energy in your body for a longer time.

Proper nutrition is vital to optimize productivity and effectiveness at work. When we nourish our body and brain with right foods, it positively affects our business and helps us remember, create, focus and accomplish any tasks in proper time.

Our brain is about 2% of our body weight however it uses 20% of calories in the body, and therefore real nourishment is necessary for it. The brain is the primary organ which helps us in the thinking process, making decisions, and that helps in focusing. Therefore it is vital to nourish it properly.

3 Sit calmly or meditate at least for 10 minutes a day

This rule seems to be very simple but has a significant impact on your productive life. A peaceful mind is a great accessory a human can have because it helps you make proper decisions at the right time and gives you the ability to think clearly.

There are several benefits you get by following this rule. This will help you decrease your stress levels and help you focus more on work, therefore, making you healthier at the mind level.

More stress levels are caused by the release of cortisol in the body which stay for a longer time and also causes several health problems. This can be overcome by meditating when you feel stressful.

When you meditate your heart requires less oxygen and therefore decreases your blood pressure.

Meditation helps to lose your weight. Weight gain is caused by cortisol production, and therefore meditation can prevent this.

Your can have improved immune system, more memory power and more ability to focus on work and have a peaceful life which is all possible by meditating. This has been proved by many great geeks and successful people.

Buddha said when asked by a man about what Buddha has gained by performing meditation daily.

Buddha replied "nothing! However let me tell you what I lost: anger, anxiety, depression, insecurity, and fear.

Meditation may not be useful in gaining but helpful in losing your bad habits very soon and losing these bad habits will automatically transform you into a real productive person.

The only goal of this chapter is to make you realize that health is more important than wealth. Without health, you can never have wealth. Give first priority to become healthy both physically and mentally, and then you could use the energy obtained from being healthy to become productive and wealthy.

Productivity secret:

      Always take healthy foods for proper health.

      Always give more importance to your health.

2. How to Deal with Interruptions and Distractions?

"There are several distractions that make you suffer failures, learn to control them."

Interruptions and Distraction are very common in life. Every living being is disturbed by some kind of disturbance and disruption on this planet. These interruptions and distractions are natural obstacles which prevent from concentration on any work you do which directly affects your productive life. Before learning more about how to control these interruptions and distractions you need to know the proper difference between these two.

Interruptions happen from the external environment which distracts you from the work you are doing. There are natural or artificial and are external in nature. These may or may not be controllable. For example, a ringing phone, change in weather, somebody knocking a door, etc., comes under this.

Distractions happen when you pay attention to interruptions. They are related or connected, but they are not equal. Distractions are artificial in nature because they are created in us when attention is paid. These are controllable and require individual's effort. The two following chains show the relation.

Interruption→Attention paid→Distraction born→Become unproductive

Interruption→no Attention paid→No Distraction born→ Become productive.

"Nothing can distract you unless you are interrupted."

If you can minimize interruptions, it becomes easy to minimize distractions because they have originated from interruptions itself. Natural interruptions are uncontrollable as they are produced by natural environment or nature such as a change in weather, rain, etc.

Artificial interruptions are generated by human or by his inventions such as mail, text message, call, and people. Therefore they are controllable by applying certain methods you are going to learn.

Researchers have shown that it takes the time to get back to work after getting distracted. On average 4-5 times an hour, a man gets distracted, and you get back to work soon to complete fast. However, these interruptions and distractions have a high impact on work life. The consequences of trying to do same work in less time are as follows:

This results in an increase in stress levels leading to mental instability.

This result in loss of interest in work you do which ultimately makes you fails at completing the work.

This lead to an increase of frustration levels which makes you hate the work you do.

There is no single perfect method which will help refrain from these interruptions and distractions. There are several methods provided by several people, but the plan that suits you is the method developed by yourself. It may be a combination of already established methods or the unique method which is very effective for you.

Many people use different methods to refrain from these productivity barriers, and every way could be the best one when used effectively.

The easiest way to prevent distractions is to have control over interruptions. When there is an active control over interruptions you will automatically prevent distractions. Interruptions are the cause of most distraction we deal with.

There was a girl, who was preparing for her exams, and she started practicing her subject on paper, and I found that she had several color pens. She began practicing again, and now she began using different pens while practicing and after writing for some time with one color pen. She began using another pen for writing. This amazed me and forced me to query about why she was doing so? So when asked about it.

She answered -I am doing so that I can refrain from getting bored and distracted.

I said what? In surprise

She smiled and answered its very simple I am getting away from distraction by creating one more distraction which is actually helping me concentrate more on my work for a longer time.

I said -a distraction to face another distraction. That's fascinating.

I said- so were you able to succeed by that way of facing distractions.

She smiled and said- yes, of course, I am able to stick to my study time more and therefore I have complete belief in this method.

And I loved the idea here. The important thing to learn from this girl is "use distraction to refrain from another distraction every time," and this rule is simple and works great when put into use. This rule may not seem to apply to you, but the method she designed for her worked well when she had put it to use, and you could develop your own method too.

We had interrogated several people who think they are procrastinators and most of them answered that lack of control over their thoughts is the main reason why they fail at accomplishing their goals, desires, and dreams.

Then they said that they have tried so many solutions but failed most of the time, and when asked whether they have applied whatever method they used to refrain from distractions effectively, most people started analyzing themselves which their silence for a while had shown us and most of them answered, No. This is what happens for most of us. We know the solution that could solve our problem, but we still don't believe in the method or fail to care about applying the method.

To be successful in accomplishing your goal, you must develop a goal or destiny in you and then you must develop a strategy and then apply it using a stepwise plan or using the principle that could help you win.

Most people in real life to refrain from internal interruptions or distractions, they try to get distracted or interrupted using another interruption which is also an effective way of dealing with interruptions or distractions.

Many people who suffer from profound sadness in their life try to avoid sadness doing some other things which may be their passionate thing or some other thing. Whatever it may be they mostly succeed in getting refrained. Even sadness is one of the interruptions which make us lose. So I think we already know how to deal with interruptions and distractions.

Even a kid knows how to get into control when distracted or interrupted because they are our internal disturbances which can be monitored when taken the proper initiative. For example, when a crying child is brought to a new place which looks attractive to the child, will stop crying after a while or suddenly which proves that changing environment is also one of the methods to control disturbances.

In this modern world, there are several distractions and interruptions which I call artificial distractions and artificial interruptions. They are really thick and are getting hold of us very tightly that we cannot easily come out of them. This is due to the advent of new technologies which made us lazy and procrastinate most of our lifetime.

In now days being away from tech gadgets are like "not a possible thing," many people feel like they are losing their freedom when they are asked to keep away from the technology at least for a little time. They are actually suggested to make them free from addiction, but they realize it because technology became essential part of their life and for few guys' life itself.

In an experiment, we called a group of people who are friends during their school days, and it's like small get together for the people. They were asked to sit in a room where they only exist, and we started noticing the people and what we found was really surprising. They spoke microscopic and only for a limited time and then suddenly they started using their mobiles, tabs, etc. Now they spoke again for a short time and then got disconnected from speech and connected to technology which makes us find the impact of technology on separating people at a high rate. This really seemed very odd as people are highly influenced by technology which made them lose control.

This experiment was taken to the next level to find out more great results of technology on individuals. We have sent our researchers to several events and asked them to find what percentage of individuals is actually socializing in the events. It is found that more than 43% people are actually out of the event mentally by being stick to tech gadgets such as mobiles, tablets, cameras, and laptops.

Our experiment proved that most distractions or interruptions in this modern world are due to tech gadgets. People know they are being distracted or interrupted by these tech gadgets, but they are not ready to refrain from them due to their addiction towards technology.

People only have control over time management when they can break this addiction habit or else they soon end as failures in accomplishing tasks.

Whatever distraction or interruption it may be you are suffering with. Your own way works just fine, and only a stable mind could have perfect control over them.

Simple methods can be used to monitor interruptions and distractions. The most important thing is to believe and act accordingly. Don't make it complicated thinking so much and if you do so, it will result in one more distraction or interruption to take place. Use simple methods which you can create by yourselves.

The girl using different color pens while practicing to get refrain from boredom, distractions, and interruptions as shared in the story above is an example of a simple method and worked well because the girl just utilized the method without thinking and it worked. You can use the girl's method by modifying in the way you want.

When suggested using a simple method to overcome the internal disturbances by people. Few people asked whether I am sure about doing so will bring out results or not. Then I told them to go on and see the change. They said as I said and not all got results, but most of the people did.

Few individuals who failed to get results are questioned about the implementation process. Most individuals who failed are suffering from mental pain due to several reasons which include family problems, relationship problems, etc. Whatever the reason may be all of them explained that they had bigger disturbances in their lives, and then I made them realize that "no problem has any size, it's all inside our brain." It is up to us who end up thinking so, and this type of thinking cannot bring any results as I expected. The only way is to think it as just as a problem leaving the terms of size big or small and then come up with solution and watch results which are the desired results.

I remembered a story to share here. One of my friends is in a deep relationship, and due to certain circumstances the relationship got spoiled, and he was doing his graduation at that time, and he was unable to concentrate on anything, and this turned evil after a particular time. He was lost somewhere mentally, and it took 3 precious years to come out of it.

After coming out of it, he realized and said that he wasted his valuable time in which he would have to get settled and have a better life, and he felt pity for himself about what he had done. Then he claimed that it is all because of thinking all the time about what happened which cannot be changed. However after getting out of the situation he has a better experience of not wasting time anymore.

From the above, it can learn that "thinking about what has already happened which could not be changed" will not bring any fruit but brings bitter moments in life. During this type of situations and many other situations in life, over thinking is what considered as a barrier or interruption. So in few circumstances of life, it's better not to think so much and just acting blindly following our soul is the best way to refrain from pain, interruptions, and distractions and have peace and stability in life. This will automatically make your life, productive life.

Productivity secret:

Face one distraction with another distraction

Use very simple techniques or methods to prevent disturbances.

3. Mental Energy is Directly Proportional to Relaxation Time

"The more you relax mentally, the more energy you will gain."

Mental energy is a most important aspect which defines our productive life behind limits. This mental energy can help you concentrate more and more for longer periods. Having right amount of mental energy is very important for maintaining control over the activities according to time. Mental energy is eternal and powerful, once you learn to gain it in you. This takes a lot of spiritual understanding than a lot of efforts.

> Mental energy gained α Relaxation time

Mental energy you gain is always directly proportional to relaxation time. This statement says that the more you relax mentally, the more mental ability you will gain. This looks simple, and when you follow the principle, your life becomes lighter and free from unnecessary things that disturb your life.

You need to understand the meaning of relaxation time first. You may be confused with this. So let me make it clear. Many people think that relaxation is nothing but getting away from the work we are dealing with and do some other stuff that will entertain us or influence us in some way by distracting us from work environment which is actually false. The important thing is relaxation time just has few moments in which you are not going to do anything but just sit and keep your mind calm which helps you obtain peace. It is kind of meditation you are going to do every time. This principle has a high impact on productive life as well as spiritual life. This helps you have more control over your life and work and also helps you maintain proper concentration for a longer time and thus helps you accomplish tasks before deadlines.

Many fruitful and happy people use this principle to gain more mental ability all the time in their productive life. This is their little secret for their success. This policy may look simple and may be hard to follow up, but with a little practice and effort, you will find success using this principle.

If you ask any satisfactory and happy person, they will tell you the impact of this principle. Let me say this man's story in which the man is really goal oriented and risk taker. He is always interested in accomplishing big things, and he was sometimes successful and sometimes not, but he was never happy. No amount of success brought him happiness which is really surprising. He was found to be always confused and in a hurry. He had no peace at all. He quit his daily job due to lack of peace in him. He had a lot of physical energy which is of course of no use as long as he cannot think clearly. Lack of mental energy made him loose things as expected. He has no success and happiness at all in his life. This is all because of lack of mental ability in him which can only be gained by proper relaxation.

This type of behavior is seen in most of the people in present situations which make them fail or become procrastinators and lose interest in life.

This man's story has a lot to teach the modern world. In this modern world most of the people have unclear thinking due to an unstable mind, and thus we see a lot of failures but if you want to be successful just learn to stay peaceful. This will help you win the situations easily and have success and happiness in life.

To find the impact of principle we did this little experiment and found surprising results. This analysis is really simple and helped in the search for the extent of usefulness of the principle. This operation is given a name called T&S test which is used to measure work efficiency in terms of time and satisfaction.

In the process, few people were selected as volunteers had been given instructions to work under four criteria and a task was assigned to them, and the task can be accomplished by anyone, and it doesn't need any expertise at all. The task is a long length in nature that is time-consuming and straightforward one.

In the first criteria, the volunteers were given instructions to work until work was accomplished and they are not allowed to take any rest. The results are noted after completion of the task in terms of time and satisfaction. The time consumed for the accomplishment of the mission is recorded based on the average of total time spent by every volunteer, and then the satisfaction feedback is taken in terms 5-star rating, and results are recorded.

In the second criteria, the volunteers were instructed to work until work was accomplished. They were allowed to take breaks frequently when they get tired or bored and in this break time they were asked to do something else that they love that is watch TV, play a game, speak to someone or anything they love which would make them feel relaxed and then they have to get back to work. At the end of the task, the results are recorded in terms of time and satisfaction as just the way it is made in the first criteria.

In the third criteria, they were assigned to work until the work is completed, and they are allowed to take breaks as in second criteria, but the exception is they have to take rest by meditating, sitting silently or taking a nap. They are not allowed to do anything else other than the mentioned relaxation tasks. At the end of the work, the results are recorded in terms of time and satisfaction as done in the above two criteria.

In the fourth criteria, the volunteers were instructed to do as in third criteria, but little changes had been made. They have take rest outside the working environment that is they have to take rest in open nature which is full of greenery, pleasant weather which is full of cool breeze, hot sun whose rays activate our internal senses. Then at the end of the task, the results are recorded as we did in above criteria.

After finalizing the experiment the results have shown as follows:

In first criteria, people have completed the task and to accomplish the task they took more time in comparison to other three criteria and satisfaction is found to be very least in this criterion.

In the second criteria, it is concluded that the time took to complete the task is less when compared to first criteria and satisfaction level is determined to be good based on average rating.

In third criteria, it is concluded that the time took to complete the task is very less in comparison to first and second criteria. Satisfaction level is considered to be mostly same as second criteria.

In the fourth criteria, it is concluded that the time took to accomplish the task is very less in comparison to above three criteria and satisfaction level is determined to be high. When people are exposed to open environment for relaxation they are highly relaxed and motivated to work more. The volunteers have actually loved the work so much and did not get tired or bored quickly showing high levels of productivity.

From the results of all the above criteria, it is clear that having mental stability and relaxed lifestyle while working is crucial for having a more productive life while working. This type of lifestyle which is highly motivating can only be attained by gaining spiritual peace and relaxed mind.

This experiment has proved the importance of mental energy gain and relaxed lifestyle while working will help you build a productive way of life.

So try to always increase mental energy which will help you succeed at accomplishing tasks in time which will help you achieve success and happiness in life.

Relaxation helps in increasing mental energy and this, in turn, helps you concentrate more on work you do.

Many big companies know the importance of relaxation, and so they provide free time to take naps for employees. Companies at present are providing rest rooms for relaxation, and this has helped the company's employees become more productive and in turn helping organizations accomplish success.

If these businesses can have a more open environment for relaxation that is exposure to nature to rest during breaks would help employees work more efficiently and in turn, helps in the motivation of workers in any industry.

This principle can be used for the personal purposes too. It can be utilized by individuals who work on their tasks or goals. What they have to do is use this principle to gain mental energy by maintaining correct exposure to open environments and getting relaxed during breaks.

When you decide to relax, I suggest you stay away from tech gadgets and move away from work environment and maintain control over time for relaxation, and this will surely make you productive. Not only this but this will also help you have mental peace which will help you become healthy mentally and have an excellent lifestyle which always free from confusion. This method also helps in gaining control over stress which is the reason for several mental disorders at modern times.

Believe in you and start exploring your happy and prosperous world. Have success in work and personal life too. This is what success is. If you have a lot of money but no happiness, money has nothing to do at all with life in the absence of joy and peace.

Productivity secret:

The more you relax mentally, the more mental energy you get.

4. Develop "Why?"

"Finding your why is very important to stay inspired and motivated."

This is most important thing to consider. This is a very simple principle which has a lot to do with. This helps in transparency over the work you do or goals you have to accomplish. This transparency helps you clear idea of what you do? Which is very essential for working effectively? All people work but not all succeed and excel at their job, and this is what happens when you have no clear idea about why you do? When you know it you will actually start loving the work and excel at things you do.

To actually succeed and become productive you must develop "why?" in you. This development of why helps you do vital tasks which you love or which you will love.

The below chains shows the importance of developing "why."

1. Work you do→know why you do? →You will love the work and success follows
2. Work you do→don't know why you do? →You will hate or compromise with work and may quit and failure follows.

The chain shows the importance of developing "Why?" which will help you develop love over the work you do.

In the 1) when you know what you do? You will love the work you do, and this will help you perform work better and helps you become productive. This principle not only just applies to the work you love but also to work you don't like. When you know why you are performing a task and knowing its end product or desired outcome of a process, you will start changing the way you look at the work you do.

In the 2) when you don't know why you do? You will hate the work you do and also may compromise with the work and soon you may end up quitting the work. Therefore it is not possible to make success and also you can never become productive all your life if you don't find "why."

So I hope you have got clear importance and idea of the principle in real life applications to become productive.

People find "Why?" in different terms when it comes to work. The "why" is found regarding money, luxury, satisfaction, happiness, family, etc. whatever the belief may be, an individual puts in; the most important thing is to believe in it firmly and act in accordance.

Whatever the term may be the ultimate "why" would be for a satisfactory and peaceful life at the end of everything we do. Everything we gain is for our mental satisfaction which is very necessary for any individual.

Everyone on this planet has hope, and it is what runs the fuel. Hope can be considered as fuel for human lives and most people "Why" developed based on hope for better future.

A friend of mine shared this story which is really inspiring. According to him, this story had taken place at a hospital. There was an old man who was working as a sweeper in that hospital. He used to clean the floor again and again as he has to keep a sterile environment in the hospital but the floor gets spoiled with dirt from shoes of visitors as they get in and out and move here and there several times. He used to get exhausted and tired due to this and used to speak to himself in bitter rage, and he hated his work.

One day as usually things were happening in old man's life at the hospital. One man who came to visit his one of his relatives got in while the old man is cleaning the floor and dirt from his shoes spoiled the floor and the old man spoke in bitter rage that these people always ruin the floor and they have no sense at all.

The man who came to visit his relative heard the old man's words and looked back at the old man and came to the old man and asked sir, what's your name? He spoke in rage and said why do you want my name? You want to complain about my behavior? Okay, you go and complain, and I don't fear of anyone.

The man smiled and said in a smooth voice that "No sir, I want to thank you for making the hospital a hygienic place." Many people come here with several diseases and when they are healed they thank doctors who treated their problems, but they never thank guys like you who are making this hospital a clean place which is very necessary. That is why I am thanking you.

The old man stood calmly for a while and looked in a pleasant manner losing his rage and maintained silence with tears in his face and said I have been doing this job for 15 years but not a single person thanked me but you are the one. The man smiled and turned back to visit his relative and he again spoiled the floor and said sorry to the old man. The old man said no problem son, don't worry. It's my job to clean it. I will take care of it, you just go. From that day the old man worked with more enthusiasm and interest, and he never got rage from that time, and he has work satisfaction from that day.

This old man story teaches us the importance of developing "why." The man who came to visit helped an old man find his "why," and that is why the old man is happy with his work. The man told about the importance of the work, the old man is doing there, and this helped the old man find the work he is doing is really prominent and a great one this inspired and motivated him to work very efficiently from that day he found his "why" of work.

Finding your, why is crucial to enjoy the work you do. In old man's case, the why is his work involves helping people by keeping the environment clean and this is imperative for a healthy environment at the hospital and he found his why paramount this is why he is happy and satisfactory remaining his life.

Finding your "why" of work is vital and finding it will help you work more efficiently and have more happiness and satisfaction from the work you do.

Don't just find your "why" Helps others to find their why too.

Productivity secret:

Find your "Why" at work to become productive.

Finding your why helps you get inspired.

5. Develop Habits That Control Your Will Power

"Habits make your willpower and willpower helps you build better habits."

Habits play a significant role in every man's life. They are what build character and attitude of an individual. Habits can transform the living ways and life itself. So they have higher influence over productive life and personal life. Habits make our time move on. There are two types of habits as we know. They are good habits and bad habits. The can be explained in the following manner.

Good habits help you succeed and have happiness and satisfaction in your life, and they grow enthusiasm, and interest in life and bad habits make you fail in every aspect of life, and they make you lose interest over life which is really awful.

Developing habits, is very easy. When you do something every day, it becomes your habit. When you don't do it regularly, you cannot grow any desired habit in you.

Creating habits is easy if you follow this method and make sure you are really interested in developing new habits. Then only you can develop habits in you which make your life productive and satisfactory.

First, decide what habit you want to grow in you and write it down on paper.

Then determine a time period in which you are going to continue pursuing the desired habit every day. For example, for a month you would follow a particular habit.

After the time period, something you are pursuing every day becomes your habit. If it doesn't happen then, extend the time period and pursue something that becomes your habit.

Only belief in change and development of your life will help you develop or change habits in you very efficiently using this method.

This process not only helps you develop habits but also to change your habits with which your life seems to be incomplete.

Let's talk about will power. Willpower is vital for having a strong desired satisfactory and productive life. This will power helps you have control over things in life. The chain goes like this.

Good Habits→Builds strong will power→Control over life

Developing good habits will help you build strong will power, and this will power helps in having better control over life, and you could become productive quickly. Understanding the chain will give you a clear idea about developing good habits and its importance in productivity. You can transform bad habits into good habits and have a better life than before.

Many people try to do several things every day but most of them fail during trials due to lack of confidence in them and therefore making a particular schedule to pursue a specific action helps you grow better habits in you, and this will surely help you grow every day and become a strong willed productive person.

As discussed will power is most important factor for having control over things and this will help you become productive. So it's the best way to have strong will power by developing healthy habits in us. This is the sure method for obtaining strong power, and the method of developing is already explained in above.

The method works perfectly if you use it correctly as explained. This is one of the guys I know, who got profited from this method in changing his habit and becoming productive.

This guy used to sit and watch TV for a long time, and he literally got addicted, and this made his lazy and unproductive. He knows that he is so lazy and unsatisfied at life doing nothing and decided to change his habit, but after several trials also he is not succeeded at all in getting refrained from the addiction.

First, he initiated a 7-day plan in which he decided to spend his 2 hours a day for doing something productive. He continued this for 7 days, and he is successful. For the next 7 days he increased the time to 4 hours in which he has to do something productive again, and for 4 weeks he continued this process, and finally he became a productive person, and he is able to lose the habit that made him lazy and unproductive. This way of developing habits starting small will have high impact in developing big will power.

Before using this method he had tried several times to change himself but he failed again and again. The reason is he said to himself he should change his habit but it doesn't happen because he tried to change the habit, at once which is not possible easily.

When he started breaking his habit starting small, he is able to break his habit and became productive and happy by being getting away from laziness that is consuming his life every day.

Habits are formed due to regular tendency or practice which are hard to give up and as something is regularly committed it becomes a habit which is very hard to give up.

As good habits start to grow in you, you will find your life interesting and very amazing. This will make you live with motivation and this, in turn, helps you become productive and successful.

This method can be used to stop or prevent several bad habits. You can use this method to stop smoking or drinking habits, stopping procrastination and avoiding junk food, etc. it may be any habit which is making you feel down, this method is sure to help you get out of it or break the habit and help you grow with ease.

The only things you have to do is start it small and go big gradually by breaking habit slowly and carefully, and it requires patience and interest to change things in life and believe in yourself which is important of all.

Productivity secret:

Develop good habits and these will build your willpower.

Willpower acts as a catalyst that speeds up the performance of any work.

6. Believe It - Time of Your Death Is Fixed

"Everyone dies someday. The very important thing to remember is, don't die in vain."

Life is really a complex thing. We take birth, and we cry, and people around us feel happy for our arrival into the world, and we die and leave this world and people around us show their sadness in the form of tears for our loss. Whatever it may be, birth and death are natural activities which happen to every organism on the planet.

Any organism it may be, the date of death of that organism is fixed, and death will happen at some point of time in life for every organism which is not possible to be controlled. Our mother nature gives us everything to live for our survival, and during death, it takes us into it. Everyone has to die someday, and there is no exception at all. This is well-known fact to every one of us who are still living in the hope of living a long lasting life which is actually an illusion.

Believe it; the time of death for everyone is fixed. We know it as fact, but we didn't accept it inside us with a deep hope of living a long life and enjoy all luxuries on earth. Whoever it may no one is ready to accept the death as a soon activity which is going to happen for sure.

I want to make this a principle which is always remembered able in your life every day. Start now with the principle in your head. Everyone is going to die someday which may happen soon or later. But take it as a rule that is you have fixed time, and no one can tell what happens in next moment of life and so work on every project you dreamt of accomplishing in your life. Spend more energy and time on fulfilling your dreams because there may not be new tomorrow to many of them. I believe that this principle has much to teach us about least amount of time we have and realizing it you have to work with full energy and enthusiasm. This isn't just a principle but a perfect statement which has influence in several people lives that are called as successful or great personalities in the modern world.

Steve job, who is founder and CEO of Apple Computers Inc said that time of death is fixed, so don't live someone's life. Don't be trapped by dogma- which is living with the results of other's people thinking. He stated that we most people live some others life which is a very pitiful thing. We waste living some others life which is also stated by several philosophers and successful men and this statement is really true and is always a barrier for a fruitful life.

Believing subconsciously this principle is very important to start living like you. You are always unique unless you want to live someone's life. Nothing can stop you when you want to really live like you, and this is what makes you the special guy and this is what life's about. Success may happen, too many of us but unique and real success happens only when you decide to live like you which unique and interesting. Life is a wonderful treasure which is uniquely gifted to every one of us and exploring it is an interesting task, and it is an only possible way to make unique success when you start living like you.

Always try to live like what you dreamt to, and this will pave a path in which you will find real productivity life and this productivity life is always interesting, satisfying and successful one for sure.

This is not at all realized by many people still in the world that is death is fixed to everyone. Let me tell one of my experiences which made my belief so stronger in this principle.

One of my friends is the highly passionate guy, and he always had big ideas and dreams, and he always wants to accomplish them at some day of his life. During our casual chats he many times used to share his ideas and dreams he wants to pursue. The days have passed by, and this unexpected thing had happened that is he is dead due to some heart problem and when I heard the news I was shocked and unable to believe it at all but it has already happened, and nothing can change it.

I felt sad for his loss, and after some days I remembered what he said about his dreams and ideas which are big and could make him great if he has actually pursued them. But he has no life now to pursue even at least one of it. I just don't know what happened and time is passing faster, and I realized that death can occur to anyone of us at some point in time. But our hope makes us live every day without worrying about death.

My friend who was dead has a well-built body but lacks proper hygienic habits. He looked alright, but his sudden death has taught so much that is death may happen soon or later. Whatever it may be we have to accomplish what we dreamt of accomplishing and waiting is a sin if we don't pursue dreams. I decided from that day I should never procrastinate on accomplishing things in life because no one knows what happens next.

Always try to finish tasks on time and stop procrastination and waiting over accomplishing your dreams and on accomplishing them you get the unlimited happiness that nothing can give you in this world.

There is one more experience shared by one of the guys I know during a regular meeting. During the meeting I spoke about this principle that is death is fixed for everyone and after the meeting, he said that he had inspired from this principle I have shared. He told that he has seen near death due to an accident which took 4 years of his life to get healed. He also added that it has taught him the importance of life and time at a time. After his recovery, he started living like actually him that is he lived his life instead of others which is what most other people do nowadays.

He added that life is really painful sometimes and only these times has much to learn and these bitter experiences teach you better lessons which are practical in nature and they are sure which will make you realize the importance of life. I am happy to hear him and thanked him for sharing his experience with me which made me grow my belief in the principle.

So, always try to live like you and always try to complete works faster. Always accomplish your goals on time, and this is all considered as productive life.

Productivity secret:

You have very limited life and work more effectively to accomplish more

Use your energy to peaks to achieve more in your life span.

7. Just Do it Strategy

"Do it today before it becomes never."

This is the approach which is used by very fewer people and who are fruitful and happy for not being late in accomplishing their actions. I have already given a brief introduction of this principle in the earlier introduction part of this book. Look for it for more about this principle.

Just do it strategy is a simple principle which has a broad range of possibilities. To make this part of your life you need to believe and act according to t this rule that is "during an act, you will either win or earn, but you will never lose. When you can make this one of your principle of life this just do it, the strategy works very well.

This strategy can also be implemented in your life when you follow the principle I have explained in 6th chapter above that is believe it the time of your death is fixed. When you believe and follow it, just do it automatically gets developed in you.

Just do it strategy is followed by only a few people, and they have the ability to take right decisions in short period of time. Many people have succeeded using this strategy and many other people have learned something from this principle. This just does it strategy should become natural part while making decisions in life and it becomes your habit when you start using it day by day when needed and to make it an effective habit in your life you could refer 5th chapter in which developing new habits effectively is being explained.

In this just do it strategy it is important to keep it in mind that logical analysis and basic thinking are very necessary without which this strategy would give you bitter fruits from every trial you perform.

This "just do it strategy" helps you get out of fear and over thinking which act as barriers to successful and peaceful life. Therefore develop just do it habit until it becomes part of every action you are going to perform.

This man Mr. X had failed to get his driving license after several trials during the test periods due to his poor driving skills. He got irritated with this and one day when asked by his friend he said that he always start thinking about the controls and everything I am going to operate, and suddenly I fail to operate the controls. The friend suggested him not to think at all and just drive with a clear mind, and this will surely help you pass the test this time, and Mr. X went to attend the test and did what his friend had suggested him to do, and he successfully passed the test which surprised him.

Sometimes over thinking leads to fear which fails us many times irrespective of n no. of trials we perform. Therefore it is better not to think and just move on that is 'don't think, just do it". Just do it strategy is useful in several areas in our lives.

This helps us make faster decisions and also helps us in winning at several opportunities in life. There are no limits unless this strategy fails to acquire basic logical analysis from us. Use this strategy well all the times with high focusing power and the results will pour out surprisingly well most of the times.

A friend of mine shared a story of an entrepreneur which acted as solid proof of this principle. He said that the entrepreneur was advised by his uncle to study hard and become an engineer. But he didn't like the advice. He is actually uninterested at studies and interested in accomplishing something big.

Then he decided to follow his heart, and he actually started a business which he never thought would be a million dollar business. But after a lot of his enthusiasm and hard work the company has grown larger and he became rich.

He said that the secret to entrepreneur's success is he just stopped thinking about other people's advice and started following his heart, and he just did it. He is able to succeed by following his heart and using just do it strategy which is great. His uncle who is always advising him started praising him now for what he is doing, and this became a happy ending.

Many people have the problem taking the initiative, and it is mainly a big problem for procrastinators and developing this strategy will help that overcome that problem. Doers follow this principle all the time, and people who support this approach are mostly risk takers, and they mostly find huge success with risk taking habit.

Developing this strategy in you is very easy when you follow this way that is whenever you want to procrastinate or want to postpone a work just stop and start doing the task at that time, and this will convert you into doers. This way may not make your success, but surely you are going to become initiative takers.

When it comes to bigger tasks, people fear of failures from this strategy. So just break the task or work into small parts and set start and end points to every small part you have broken and start performing every part at a time, and this will help you lose your fear of failure while doing a bigger task using this strategy.

Following this strategy helps you get relieved from fear, over anxiety, overthinking and create a need for urgency in every work you do. Therefore it could save you from increased stress levels in your life. This strategy has high importance in developing do it now attitude development in individuals.

There is no some complex solution to develop this habit, and this habit or attitude can only be developed with a keen interest in you to become a highly productive person. This strategy helps you become very productive as you will become the initiative taker at every task you are going to accomplish and this will help you become highly productive, and you live beyond limits of several barriers to success.

This method or strategy is the secret of most successful people who have "do it now" attitude, and they are successful, and risk takers and you could be too if you are ready to develop just do it attitude in you. This strategy can be used in several areas which may include small areas too. Everything becomes easy to work on when you can develop this attitude in you.

Productivity secret:

Never think too much before you do anything.

Just do it approach helps you develop to do it now a habit.

Never fear of anything if you want to be a doer.

8. Moment of Inspiration is an Illusion Unless You Start Pursuing An Action

"Don't just sit and wait for your turn, try grabbing an opportunity and start working before its too late."

This should be understood clearly before you take any more decisions in accomplishing any task from now. This secret will explain much about the failures caused to many people nowadays and therefore knowing this helps you become to realize the truth and act as soon as possible.

This principle states that moment of inspiration is an illusion unless you start pursuing an action. Only a few lucky people who know their true passion are an exception to this principle just for a little time. Many people wait for the moment of inspiration and waste their time doing nothing but just waiting, and they are losing their valuable time by doing so.

So it's better for many of you to pursue any action and move on and search for inspiration in what we do. If you have a strong passion, go for it or else just go on with work and search for inspiration.

These two guys X and Y stories would teach us so much about the importance of principle. The guy x is interested in big pictures, and he is interested in something big, and he is waiting for time. He had a good job that pays him well, but he quit it due to lack of interest in the job and tried several things. But mostly failed and the time has come for the settlement, but due to several failures he was unable to get settled and thus lost most of his precious years that made him lost everything including financial security, peaceful life, etc.

As he waited for the moment of inspiriting without having any clear passion in him made him lose his precious time which he will never get at all. This guy's story teaches about the importance of time and loving the work we do unless we have a particular passion for something else.

The guy y is different from guy x where guy y is not a waiting type guy. He does whatever work he got, and he loved the work he does. He is inspired by the work he does and thus got success from the job he does. He is also a guy who is passionate, but he never waited for the moment of inspiration. He got paid well for the job and used what he earned for accomplishing his big goal.

Here the two guys' stories could relate to many of them, and these stories teach us the importance of not waiting for the moment of inspiration, and the longer you wait for it, the most valuable time you will lose and as a result, you will have an unsatisfied life which is unstable.

Always be wise in taking decisions. It's wise decision to pursue an action and search for moment of inspiration rather than wasting time just on waiting for moment of inspiration

The longer you wait for the moment of inspiration; it will become an illusion soon in which you are going to lose your valuable time and energy. So it's better you stay in the present and love your work you do first.

Productivity secret:

Never sit and wait to do nothing

Always pursue some action, and this will help you learn new things in life.

You will become lazy and a procrastinator if you keep waiting for the moment of inspiration.

9. Use Limited Time and Unlimited Energy

*"Never share this secret to anyone.
You have limited life but not limited energy."*

Have you ever realized the importance of time which is limited we have? But of course realization of this may make people hurry at doing things, and this result in failures and therefore one more thing has to be realized along with it. One more thing you have to realize is you have unlimited energy. Understanding this will help you get refrained from the point that is we have limited time and helps us in working with full energy in accomplishing things. So this works as a thumb rule for working faster than before.

We got very limited time which ends very soon at some point, but we have unlimited energy which we can use to accomplish things faster than before. So use your limited available time to accomplish tasks faster utilizing your unlimited energy.

Limited time refers to our living time which is different for different people. The anonymous truth to everyone is that how much time each individual has? Therefore stop waiting and start working to fullest with full energy utilization and this will help you win in every situation at accomplishing tasks.

This near old man story has a point to consider. The man used to work hard using his full energy, and he is multi-tasked, and he works for a long time with full concentration over work. He is successful and happy with his work. He on enquiring answered that he is highly passionate about his life and he always wants to be more productive and to make the things happen he made this his principle at work.

He is working hard now using the energy he has now to get fruits or results which are desired. In future or near future as he grows up he may not be able to work to fullest level as he is working such way now. In future, he may not have energy which he has now and so he decided to work now and create secure future life.

He is very true that most people waste time waiting and soon their energy levels go low as they become older and they may not have full energy to utilize in accomplishing tasks. Therefore it's better to realize it and act now to have a secured future life.

Many people know this, but not many people become productive knowing this which is really pitiful. We have very limited time to live here, and in such limited time, we have very less time for a relaxed and secure life. Combining all it's better to act at our works to full and earn a better life for tomorrow.

The near old man who knows this point has worked to become productive and secured. He used to work as a clerk in the morning time and in the evening he used to work for a part time job, and he is never relaxed and kept working for long hours and gained fruits for future.

Like this man, there are several people who really want a secured future life, but not everyone works for it. Many people lack interest and enthusiasm in their lives, and this is why they fail most of the time. This is the reason why people are not productive and unsuccessful.

Therefore use the time you have now in accomplishing the tasks using your full energy levels you got and these energy levels are rechargeable and so work to your fullest, and this will help you become a productive person.

There are so many tasks which have to be repeated in our everyday lives, and these tasks require high energy levels, and they are time-consuming. Therefore find ways to make these tasks simple, so they require less time and energy levels.

There are two types of energy, physical and mental energy. Using the physical energy, you can do few tasks and by using your mental energy you could do few more tasks and by using both the energies you can do many more tasks.

Example for mental energy could be an invention that minimizes time consumption and efforts in accomplishing a particular task. This invention is only possible when you can use your enormous mental energy. This will help you accomplish tasks faster, and they consume fewer efforts.

There are several machines invented in the modern world created through this principle by people, and this principle is stable and natural one, that has the capacity to provide some great fruits or results.

Believe me, you can do wonders when you realize that you have unlimited energy and make use of energy in completing tasks on time. Many people think that it is not possible to have success by just realizing and this is true to a limited level.

Always have faith in your energy levels, and this will help you concentrate more on work and complete it faster. This energy required for completing tasks faster can be obtained by many ways.

Physical energy can be gained by taking proper and healthy diet, and mental energy can be gained by several ways. One way is already explained in chapter 2 that is the most relaxed you are, the more energy you can gain.

There are several other ways to get high energy in us. Few get it by others encouragement, and few people get it through inspiration and few others get it by some other unexplainable ways.

Whatever it may the most important thing is to realize this principle and act accordingly. Nature can provide us enormous energy, and this helps us complete tasks within our lifespan, and this is very important for witnessing our satisfied living, and this is what makes our lives complete.

Use your physical energy only when it's necessary and use your mental energy to minimize efforts by creating simple processes and minimizing steps of a process wherever possible, and this will help you consume more time in accomplishing tasks and also helps in minimizing the efforts. Energy is renewable and time isn't. So use your time very wisely and use your energy accordingly in accomplishing tasks.

Always create a balance between limited time and unlimited energy to accomplish more in life which is a productivity sign.

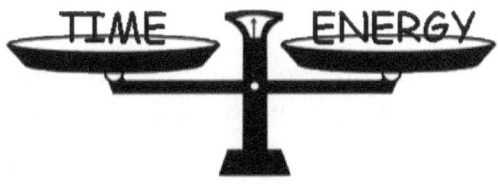

Balance time and energy for best results

Productivity secret:

Always use your full energy to accomplish your goals and dreams.
You have very limited time and unlimited energy.

10. How to Gain Self-Control?

"Self-control is most difficult and if you can acquire it, you can control anything."

Self-control is a vital aspect of becoming productive, successful and happy. Lack of self-control is the reason for most of the sorrows the human are suffering with. Having self-control will help you win the world where you have the powerful influence on time and situation.

Many successful men, saints, and sages know the importance of self-control, and they have become greater influencers. The most difficult task is to have the control you. If you can do it, you can have control over anything. Therefore it is very important to have self-control if you wish to be successful and productive all your life.

Having self-control helps you get refrained from procrastination. It also helps you free from stress. Self-control can cure many problems human are dealing with in the modern world.

Self-control is the ultimate way of influencing the world through controlling yourself. Having self-control helps you have a satisfied life. Lack of self-control is the reason for pain in human life in most of the situations. Even in the case of productivity, the lack of self-control is a greater barrier that is impossible to conquer.

This self-control chain helps you understand the importance of having self-control in our lives. This chain helps you figure out why many people in the modern world lose interest and hope to the beautiful life they have.

1. Have self-control→self-respect increases→life is interesting and hopeful with positive energy.
2. Have no self-control→self-respect decreases→life is boring and hopeless with negative energy.

The two above chains can explain the difference between having self-control and lack of self-control. Take any successful or great personality on this planet. Everyone has one thing in common that is they have self-control, and it is what keeps their lives creative and innovative every day.

Having self-control will enhance self-respect and this, in turn, increases interest over one's own life, and this will make their lives hopeful and helps people realize the importance of life, and this has a direct effect on the way of living which has an impact on people around us.

When you can gain self-control, it becomes easy to manage anything easily. Time is an uncontrollable factor which is considered to be very important, and you can gain control over time by having self-control, and this will make you productive.

Self-control makes you productive by minimizing stress, interruptions, and distractions in life. Gaining self-control is not so easy in this modern distractive world where illusions rule our brains.

The only way to gain self-control is to free yourself from illusions, and this will help you have a peaceful mind which is an important asset to gain self-control.

People who seem to be peaceful have great self-control, ask them, and they will tell you. Many people including Buddha, Gandhi, Vivekananda, etc. are successful and happy by enlightening the world are the one who has greater self-control.

This self-control acts at every step we take every day. Starting from, wake up from the bed. Many people of modern times have the habit of getting up late or sleeping very late and have less amount of sleep, and this causes several health problems and having self-control helps you win this situation.

Apply this self-control principle for time management, and you could have better managing habit over time in no time. Self-control helps you get refrained from things that make you procrastinate and therefore helps you accomplish tasks on time.

One of my article readers regarding self-control approached me and shared his experience regarding how he got inspired by my writing. He said that he is unhappy and sad for several years due to lack of interest over life which is due to several successive failures happened in his life.

He said that he realized that the cause of failures is due to lack of self-control. He expanded that he always hurries at doing things and taking decisions. This made him fail several times. Gradually he lost self-respect which happened due to failures, and then he got bored of living due to increased negative thoughts in him, and this is why he has several suicide thoughts, and after realizing the truth, he started changing himself and started making a real life which is successful and happier. I have explained the chain of self-control above which gives a clear idea of self-control and its importance.

Getting habituated with the habit of self-control will help you have more control over things in life and time is one among them and when you gain control, you will have freedom of living with high energy every day and get success by accomplishing any task.

A small firm's manager asked how he can manage employees to come on time to the office without being late. He said that employees who come late to office are really a mess and this will inevitably affect the productivity and growth level of the business. There are many people who come to office late, and the manager asked for a creative and permanent solution.

Then he has been assigned a simple task to perform. He had given instructions to make rating cards and distribute to the employees in which employees has to give a genuine rating on the grade of 1 to 10. If they come on time, they have to grade 10, and if they are late, they have to grade less than ten based on how much late they come. This has to be done for 15 days. Then average rating of each individual has to be made and submitted on the 16th day, and these results are shared with all employees with a note saying "you have done well and try more." It is found that about 27% of employees are late most of the time.

To control this, for the next 15 days, the employees are said to rate themselves the same way they did in last 15 days. But now they have to show improvement by decreasing the late time and rating has to go up. Not all guys did well from this experiment, but a couple of guys have done well by this experiment. They started coming to office on time, and they said that they got irritated of rating themselves less than others, and therefore they decided to change themselves and they said self-control helped them win this situation. They expanded that every day they rated themselves they decided to have increased rating every day.

So a guy of two said that the stronger decision he took helped him the habit of coming to office on time every day. But another guy has a strategy which helped him overcome the late habit. He said that he controlled 10 minutes a day in the early morning and this gradually helped him overcome the late habit.

He stated that he decided to take a small initiative that is complete things 10 minutes before every day and this helped in saving more and more time every day in which he can have more free and peaceful life in dealing things. He added that after using this strategy, he never rushed into things every morning. He has got freedom from tension and stress and able to complete tasks on time. The progress is marked every day, and the rating card helped him increase the habit of being on time.

Self-control cannot be obtained at a time at once. It is the progressive type which takes time and efforts. The way second guy uses the progressive type strategy using which he gained self-control and control over time which made him successful and productive. Self-control has a wide range of applications in everyday lives of modern people without which the people are suffering so much. They need to learn to start small and grow self-control in them.

Self-control can help you overcome addictions which kill productivity. Addiction to something whatever it may be. It could be watching TV, chatting habit, browsing the internet for a longer time and sleeping too much, etc. self-control can solve most of the issues that deal with addiction.

Self-control is a habit, and this guy developed it this way which is very simple but effective. This guy has the habit of speaking so much on mobile. Sometimes the talk goes for several hours, and he always wants to get rid of this addiction, but he failed after several trials. This is because he tried to stop it at once which is no possible and not so easy. So he is being advised to break the addiction starting small.

He has to minimize speaking on the phone starting 15 minutes a day initially. For the first few days he has minimized 30 minutes of speaking time and then slowly the speaking time of 2 hours is minimized and this gradually continued, and at the end, he started speaking whenever necessary, and he broke his addiction which kills his productive life. Taking small steps helps you win for sure. Patience is what matters the most for breaking bad habits and gain self-control.

There may be several methods which help you gain self-control, but the methods made by you for you works great than any method. Always have confidence in you and stay in control to make yourself productive. Productivity is getting better every day and therefore every small change in life, adds up to your productive life.

Productivity secret:
> Self-control can help you have control over time which is very important to become productive.
>
> Self-control can be gained by controlling your mindset.

11. How to Complete any Task Faster?

"Sometimes speed is a factor that states success."

The fast represents accuracy and speed here, not hurry or rushing in accomplishing things. Do you know what drives us to accomplish any task faster? Did you ever enjoy saving a little time and having freedom of life? So now it's time to get down into the ways to become faster at work which drives your productive life.

The only thing that drives speed is will power. Willpower is what dictates the speed of task. Developing strong willpower helps you to accomplish tasks, and this can be clearly understood by the following equation and its explanation.

The equation you are going to learn is called as inspiration as catalyst equation found through one of our experiment which drives you to develop will power and accomplish tasks very fast than before.

Willpower is directly proportional to the speed at which a task is accomplished, and inspiration acts as a catalyst in the equation.

$$\text{Willpower} \propto \text{speed at which a task is finished}$$

In the above equation, inspiration acts as a catalyst which speeds up the process of acquiring willpower which in turn enhances the speed of work.

The experiment which gave this equation is as follows. In the experiment, a group of people who lack interest in their work is selected and they were given a task to perform and the time taken to complete the task are noted. Along with time the individuals are instructed to genuinely rate the amount of willpower they have on a scale of 1 to 10. This is the first stage, and the results are recorded and analyzed.

In the second stage the same group of people from the 1st stage are selected and allowed to do the same task, but in between the 1st and 2nd stage, the people were exposed to inspiration. The group of people is inspired to gain will power in them by exposing them to few inspiring presentations and videos and then is made to work without any late. This experiment gave surprising results and people who hate their work accomplished the task faster than before, and their willpower is also increased which is found from their rating. Every individual has unlimited willpower, but we made them realize it through catalyst called inspiration and then we have seen best results than before.

Inspiration is one of the catalysts of developing will power useful in enhancing your willpower, and there are several catalysts you could use to enhance your willpower and accomplish tasks. This inspiration as catalyst equation could be useful in developing an interest in any work you do. This will help you become more productive at work. So start using this simple equation at becoming a very productive person. Inspiration can be found from several places. It exists everywhere. What you have to do is discover it and when it's found you will start loving the way you work and live. I suggest you search inspiration from your around sources for faster results. Don't keep searching if it is hard to find it just keep doing your work with more enthusiasm and some day you will find it in you.

There are several ways you could accomplish your works faster, and there will be several more ways in the future. People keep finding new and innovative ways to finish tasks faster and easier. Human laziness and enthusiasm act as support components for new discoveries and inventions which help in doing more in less time using fewer efforts

One of my good friends explained his way of doing any work faster. I call this way, time limiting strategy which is very simple in nature but worth one for utilizing in completing tasks faster. According to the strategy to complete a task as we know requires a certain amount of time. So my friend used to set a time limit for a task which is usual one for us, and he minimized the amount of time a task requires and tries to accomplish in less time than it requires. He may not be successful every time, but mostly he won it. This way, he experimented with time and learned to perform better and faster. This technique looked very simple but when put into use shown successful results. You can use this strategy to minimize the amount of time a task requires. This strategy helps you grow challenging power in you.

Any task requires a particular amount of time but the time is fixed thought is a mental illusion. Breaking this barrier and moving on with the work will surely help you accomplish tasks faster.

Break the barriers technique is one of the ways to finish tasks faster. We know any work we do has restrictions which take off precious time in the process. When you can prevent these barriers, it becomes easy to complete work faster. There are several barriers which include interruptions, distractions, addictions, procrastination, and laziness, etc. whatever the barrier may be the result is they affect the amount of time and energy a task requires to get done.

It is already explained that is about preventing interruptions and distractions in the above initial chapters. Whatever that comes in your way while accomplishing things are considered as barriers, and the important thing is to learn to control or prevent them by some way to become productive and complete works faster.

This lady who is a student of mine had developed a way to manage these barriers and work faster. She uses the technique called kill one at a time to prevent work barriers. She notes down the barrier of her work and finds a solution and solves the barrier that makes her work late. Then she controls every barrier one at a time and makes work move faster than expected. This helped her become more productive at whatever work she does.

Every one of us is brought down by some barrier in life. If you can realize, what is it that is holding you down and find a better solution for it. You will easily become faster at work and become productive.

Accomplish your works, goals or dreams faster, and this helps you become productive and successful.

Productivity secret:

Willpower helps you accomplish more in less time.

Inspiration acts as a catalyst to grow more will power.

12. How Every Small Task Counts?

"Every small task has to be done if you want to be productive."

Have you ever measured the size of task? Many people do it. What is the scale for measuring the size of work? Is it time? Or is it just our mindset? Answers to these questions will give your clear idea of this chapter and helps you realize the importance of every task you do every day.

Many people measure the size of the task and then set priorities to different tasks, and this is wrong way of doing tasks. It's okay to set priorities and then perform but make sure this doesn't become a habit. When you start measuring tasks, you will start setting priorities and then you will start postponing few or more tasks for later, and soon procrastination rules your productive life and makes it unproductive and boring.

You have to realize this important thing to change your mindset of measuring tasks. The important thing is there is no measuring unit for task measurement, and it is our mindset we have grown till now that makes you measure the size of a task. Therefore come out of this illusion and stop setting priorities and sizes to tasks and start doing any task which you may call small, big, greater or unimportant. Whatever name you would give to task the important thing is to do it now without postponing.

Many people postpone tasks thinking that are small but at the end they become the biggest and difficult task you have to finish. So it's better to realize it now and act as fast as possible or else you will end up doing work which you will hate sooner.

The reason why people start hating the work is due to setting the size and priorities to work. This will decrease your interest over particular tasks and this, in turn, grows hate over the work, and you will soon end up not doing that particular work anymore. This is why many people lose their interest in doing certain tasks. So stop measuring tasks and setting priorities.

A student approached me after a speaking session, and she shared his problem with procrastination. She had the habit of postponing the works. She postponed her work, again and again, every day and this made her lose control over the work, and she asked for a solution.

This is not only her problem but many of you in the modern world. Many people postpone tasks they have to accomplish today itself to tomorrow and tomorrow's tasks to some other day, and this continues. As a result, these people lose control over the work and search for shortcuts and end up feeling stressful.

I have shared one of my friend's stories with the student who approached me for a solution. My friend told me one day that he had to give a small presentation in a week about nanotechnology at his college. He decided to prepare it and rehearse so much so that he can give it effectively. On 2nd day he did not start making his presentation and when asked he said he got so much time to make it. He postponed it again and on the 4th day he said that he has two more days to make it, but he did not do it.

The day has come that is there is only one day remained for making and rehearsing the presentation, and he suddenly started feeling stressful and started doing it in a great hurry as time is very limited. He finally finished the presentation and did a rough rehearsal.

He is still feeling stressful as he is not sure about how many mistakes he's going to make. Finally, the day has come where he has to present his presentation. He started shivering on the stage, but soon he recovered and gave his presentation. He came back and said that he is happy for not making many mistakes. He also said I thought I would complete the presentation within less time as it is a small one but it took me a lot of time for completion.

I smiled and answered that he is right. He would have done better if he had started doing more early and he would have not made that mistakes he did. I asked him what the reason for postponing the presentation making is. He said that it is a small presentation and that is why he postponed it.

I told him that there is no scale to measure a task whether it's a presentation or any other task. Measuring the size and setting priority made you lose interest in completing the presentation and this way you have grown stress in you at the end and made mistakes.

My friend smiled and said that I am true and he also told that he will never judge the size of a task and never sets priority. Then after his decision, he started completing tasks more efficiently.

After sharing this story with the student, I asked her whether she understood the solution. She smiled and said well yes and she asked, what's more, she has to do. I told her to stop measuring the size of tasks, and so that she will have no priorities and she can give equal importance to every task she does which will enable her to work equally for every task.

Many people cannot refrain from judging the task by size. Therefore another way to perform each and every task is to create or induce a belief of every small work counts and believe in the importance of any task, and this will help you get refrained from setting particular priorities.

Small tasks include everything which may be cooking, cleaning, traveling, shopping, and talking, etc. There are no limits. Whatever task it may be, start doing it with full interest, and this will help you become a productive person.

The thinking of small task and give priorities also affected several businesses and entrepreneurs' success. In our research, it is found that the reason for the failure of several entrepreneurs and small businesses is due to a decrease of interest which happened because of considering what they are doing as small work or task.

It's all in the mindset that is limiting our thinking and making live us in the illusions from which it is not easy to get out and gain success. Thinking any task as small makes you lose interest and therefore it's better to get out of it and start working on everything with whole heart and full concentration. This will force your heart to love anything you do from now on.

One more additional tip is finished every task which requires just minutes of time, and this will help you complete small tasks before they become a bulk set.

Productivity secret:

Do every small task that comes in your way.

Do every task immediately which consumes only minutes of time.

13. Smart Cuts Will Help You Perform Better

"Be smart to make or use smart cuts to gain success."

What are these smart cuts? How they will help you? How to create or find them? How will they help us in finding efficient ways? Providing answers to these questions will help you have a clear idea of smart cuts and thus helps you become productive.

Have you ever heard of shortcuts? Of course, many of us know them. So now it becomes easier to understand these smart cuts. Smart cuts are the amplified or improved shortcuts which are very effective when used. Smart cuts are far better than shortcuts.

Shortcuts follow status quo but smart cuts won't. Smart cuts challenge status quo and makes huge success that gives you more satisfaction and happiness. Smart cuts are of different kinds, and they are most innovative and effective.

Consider all these as smart cuts that include weird techniques, upgraded shortcuts, innovative ideas, process that has least steps, a unique idea or technique that has come to existence, an invention that reduces human efforts, etc.

Many successful people including artists, overnight movie stars, top selling authors, writers have used these smart cuts to outrun their peers. These smart cuts can also help you perform better and make you very productive. Even you all know several people who got overnight success or fast success which is still surprising to everyone. They all used one thing in common, and I call them smart cuts.

Let me show the relation between smart cuts, productivity and success and the relation can be easily understood by the following linear chain.

Use Smart cuts→High productivity→big success

Using smart cuts help you to perform better which is considered as productive, and the outcome of being productive is a success. Now you have understood the importance of smart cuts in becoming productive.

Only people who have enthusiasm and passion can become innovative and creative, and only these people can make effective smart cuts which give better results. Start being enthusiastic and passionate about any work you have to perform and it becomes easy to accomplish any work at ease.

In an experiment, five people who are expertise at something are selected, and they were given instructions to write a shortcut method which worked for them in which they are expertise at, and they are also instructed to prove it as a shortcut method which actually works. After completing the certain tasks using the shortcut methods the time and enthusiasm levels are noted.

Now the real magic was ready to happen. These 5 experts were told to develop their shortcuts that are the shortcut methods they are using should be upgraded somehow. They were given a certain amount of time to develop the methods and then submit the improved methods and prove the efficiency of those methods. The results are better than results from shortcuts. Now they were enquired about how they are able to upgrade them and bring more efficient results.

They said one thing most in common that is they have become experts in certain subjects in which they are highly interested in and passionate about therefore nothing looked hard for them while upgrading the methods. They also said that this experiment helped them reinvent the ways they are already using and they are happy with it.

They also shared some important things of the process in which they are able to transform shortcuts to smart cuts. They said that shortcut is also a process which has several steps to be followed in completing a task. However, it is against the standard process of completing a task. However, these shortcuts save a lot of time and increase one's interest in particular tasks that have to be accomplished.

It's not so easy to transform shortcut to smart cut because shortcut itself is the efficient way which we thought. But during the experiment, we are able to minimize the steps required in the process of completing a task using shortcuts and then save more time. They also said that they learned that it's all their mindset that have set limits to their methods and they have learned to break them. They also said that sometimes transformation of the shortcut is not possible so there is a need to pick up a completely random method which is more efficient than the before method which can be considered as smart cuts.

So you could make your own smart cuts by transforming existing shortcuts or picking up some other new method which can be effective. So use the principle of minimizing the number of steps or brainstorm for a completely new idea of making things happen fast and effective.

As I told you earlier that smart cuts helped many people become successful in a very short period of time. They all has done something in common that is they all had done something really crazy that no one has ever done till date and this is what brought success to those people, and you could become one of them with a crazy or innovative idea. This type of way could be called as smart cut way.

There are several barriers in our lives which hold us back again and again from getting success, but sometimes it's very hard to overcome them and so use these smart cuts to become free from the barriers that hold you back and get succeeded.

Smart cuts will improve your way of working and helps you complete tasks faster and make you productive. They save a lot of time and energy. Many inventions of this modern world could be considered as smart cuts taking from coffee the machine to rocket. Whatever that minimizes human efforts and helps him save more time is a part of the smart cut. Generally, many of us use these smart cuts in our daily life in this modern world, and you could start making your own ones from now.

Productivity secret:

        Smart cuts are upgraded form of shortcuts.

They are weird ways to which you gain success within very short time.

14. Stay Action-Oriented

"Actions can speak more loudly than words."

Staying action-oriented is very important if you want to become very productive at whatever you do in life. Many successful people and productive people are action oriented. Many people fail at becoming action-oriented and therefore fail to be productive. There are barriers, that make you fail. Becoming action oriented is not easy unless you change your mindset system. How to become action oriented? What are its barriers? These questions are answered to give you clear idea of becoming action oriented. This topic is connected to few chapters we have discussed initially, and therefore it's better not to skip any forward chapters.

There are several barriers which prevent you becoming action oriented and understanding the barriers gives you ways to become action oriented and productive. The barriers are fear, addiction, laziness, over speech, over thinking, procrastination, etc. These are most common barriers most people are suffering with. Overcoming these barriers will surely make you action oriented in no time.

Most of the barriers are mental related barriers and therefore it's time to change your mindset to change everything in your life. Fear is the biggest barrier to any success. The only way you could get rid of it is to just face it. Many people skip some things due to fear, and this brings them the pain of failure. These people are non-risk takers. They have a fear of failures, and they don't take risks, and they quit things which make them fail most of the time. They fail at becoming action oriented and productive.

Fear is the cause of all errors in life and fear is the cause of all evil in your life. When you can realize it with your wisdom, your life becomes happier and successful. Becoming productive has several constraints and fear is one of them and overcoming it has surprising results in real life.

Becoming action oriented is a permanent habit for real successful people, therefore, to induce it as a permanent habit, high enthusiasm and will power are very necessary and belief in you is the great catalyst for speeding up the process of becoming action oriented. We have already learned about making habits and will power in the initial chapters. Take a glance to have a more clear idea about them.

One of my senior during post graduation had the problem of fear in his life which limited him from getting a job. So many people have a fear of interviews, and he is one among them. He has got several job offers and being called for attending interviews, but most of the times he never showed up due to fear. He almost wasted about two and half years just receiving the job offers, and he never shared his fear with anyone and knocked down every opportunity he received.

The days passed by and the day has come where he has to earn money to make his family survive which had happened due to his father death, and he started selling fruits just like his dad did to run his family. He is postgraduate, and his fear made him as not important being a postgraduate, and he still sold fruits to run their family. He is being advised by several people to do a job, but he never listened to anyone but actually the fear made him not to hear anything from others. So many days passed by and he still sells fruits and the fear in him increased so much that he is not even ready to face anything anymore.

When enquired he said that the cause of increased fear is due to the time period he had wasted till date. He felt very sad for neglecting the job offers he had due to fear of failure. On forcing him to attend interviews by preparing well, he started to try things and then he got a small job somehow and got settled. Loss of fear made him pass the interview and acquire a job.

There are so many people who had a fear of interviews, and that is how they even though well qualified for the job remaining unemployed and ending up doing some other jobs. Most of them are not ready to become the part of the competition which seems to be a real risk for their success.

The loss of fear is only possible when you take the initiative. I call this the initiative of facing the fear of anything. Whatever makes you feel fear is evil and destroy that evil in your life? This will help you overcome the biggest and worst barrier to success in your life. Never ever allow your fears in you speak out, and it is courage which must speak louder. Fear makes you lose a lot of valuable time, and this is you will become unproductive.

Addictions also act as barriers to becoming action oriented and learn to break them which will be explained in further chapters. There are several traits which tell whether you are action oriented or not.

Action oriented type people and fewer speech people and more working people, and they know the real value of time. They speak less, and they are considered as introverts mostly by people. But the truth is they are extroverts, and they love talking to people but only what is useful. Try researching successful people, and you will find their traits which made them action oriented.

Try using "just do it approach" repeatedly which is already explained in the earlier chapters, and it will help you become action oriented and productive. Fear of failure has to be ejected out from you to make the approach your habit.

You are what you speak, and you are judged by "how much" and "what" you speak? People judge you by those two factors and your inner-self also judges you on those two factors. So be careful while speaking.

Make your actions speak and not your words. Your actions bring more effective results than your words. Speak less and act more should be your principle of life for getting productive. Many people have the habit of speaking so much, and they feel it hard to break that habit.

Therefore this way of assessment will help you break the habit. Start whether "what" factor is logical or not. If yes you can speak and if not just don't speak it at all. When you practice logical analysis of "what" it becomes easy to decrease "how much" factor, and this will help you speak less and act more which is considerable to be important for becoming productive.

Always stay action-oriented to get things done and have a productive and successful life.

Productivity secret:

Continuous use of just do it approach helps you develop to do it now a habit, and this will make you, action oriented.

15. Crafting Effective Plan

"Planning is a process and plans are its output."

Planning is a very important step of any process. Sometimes the whole success depends on it. Do you why planning is very important? Do you know why even greater plans fail? There are several things you should be aware about the importance of crafting effective plans. Planning is a process which requires several factors that include subject knowledge, logical skills and keen interest. These are primary factors for any plan, and even greater plans are made considering those factors. Even though they are greater plans, they also fail many times.

These greater plans also lack certain factors, and they are enthusiasm and passion. Along with the primary factors the factors mentioned will give more strength to an effective plan. Many people plan to accomplish things to produce desired results, but the results are not always as expected.

The plans are made based on certain conditions and this makeup of plans follow a process for obtaining more results. Any process that has certain limits cannot be considered as effective and therefore not every plan made is effective. Use a lot of enthusiasm and passion for making effective plans. Creativity is what missing from every plan made these days. Many plans are made based on complicated frameworks which are not always fit for every plan we make.

We know that particular frameworks don't work well every time we make plans, but we still follow them blindly because we don't like making new frameworks which we feel consumes a lot of time. When you have enthusiasm and passion for completing something you make some random creative plans which mostly gives you desired results as well as satisfaction.

Crafting effective plans do not follow status quo, and it actually challenges and overcome status quo and bring out unexpected, surprising positive results. These types of plans are made by successful people who are enthusiastic and passionate about accomplishing things. Artists, ad makers, writers, authors, passionate businessmen, etc. follow this way of planning.

In this context effective plan doesn't mean that has complicated framework but the one who can give effective results. The plan may look very simple, but if it gives better results, it can be considered as effective plan.

Effective plan → produce effective satisfactory results

Many viral ads, best artworks, books or successes gained are only made possible by effective planning. Even effective plans lead to success that happens within a short time. The main feature of effective planning is it's mostly simple to execute, and it always works great giving results as expected. It is also less time consuming and it minimized human efforts. So grow the two factors in you while planning and you could make the best plan which is simple to execute and pours results as expected.

Crafting effective plan is easy for passionate people because they have no fear of failure and they always have a free mind which is full of positive thoughts, and thus results are also positive because we are made up of our thoughts and success is based on how we think and act.

The easy way to craft the effective plan is to stick to the existing plan and upgrade it or improve it. This way you can develop an effective plan from scratch. This will help you stick to the framework of the plan you already have and improving it will make it the effective plan which is easier than creating a new plan which has a new framework.

Effective plans give you desired results which show you as productive. Crafting effective plans do follow any pattern, but they also contain steps or limits at a basic level while getting constructed. An effective plan can be made only when you have enthusiasm and passion for accomplishing something.

To find out why plans fail we have done an experiment. We have selected a group of people, and they were divided into two groups based on high success rate with planning group to low success rate with planning group. Now after division people from two groups are interviewed about their planning habits and results are recorded.

Surprising answers have been found from the interviews and what lacks people from low success rate with planning is, enthusiasm and interest as we have thought, but it isn't just it, but also these people are lazy internally and never believed in changing themselves to become successful people. They want things to happen easily in their life that is they want easy success, easy cash, an easy life which is not possible at all.

From the answers of people who have high success rate with planning, it had been found that planning is a very important aspect of accomplishing anything. Believe planning is the vital part of completing tasks fast and easy.

From the results, it is found that giving first priority to planning will enable us to focus more on future aspects and makes it easy to complete things. People who can have real hopes for future are better planners. There is no easy way to finish tasks. Any task you feel very important can only be accomplished by an effective plan. Effective plans are easy to make if you concentrate on end results.

While starting the plan just write down what you want to accomplish that is what is the outcome you are expecting from a particular task. Use posters on which the end result is written with your hand or printed and place it everywhere in your room where your sight goes most of the time. This way helped many people plan properly and get desired results. This one simple technique has greater impact when care is taken. This will always make you remember the plan for accomplishing that particular thing you want to accomplish.

For example, you wished to have 1000 dollars within a period of 15 days. Just write it down the plan you are going to make and make a poster of it and place it on the wall. Now find all the ways how you earn that amount and write down the plan stepwise for effective execution and start with the work with no more waiting. This will surely help you becoming productive by gaining whatever you wished to have in a particular period of time. We have implemented this technique during few of our whole week sessions in different places and found desired results as we expected.

Even this guy proved our point. This guy wants to plan better and get success from every plan he planned. He asked for advice and then he is being instructed to write down whatever he wants to gain in life on a sheet of people. Along with his wishes, he has to write maximum time that his plan will take to fulfill his wish. Now he is asked to filter the wishes list he made. Now he has to make a list in which has to write most important things he wants to accomplish in life and they should be only three wishes in the filtered list. Now time has to be noted beside the three wishes on the list.

He is asked to make plans which should be effective enough and in a while he made plans and started explaining how he is going to accomplish three biggest things of his life and he also added that these three wishes take very much time. Then he is being instructed to minimize the amount of time which is not possible according to him. When asked whether he is sure to complete those things in mentioned time on the list. He said maybe. Then it's time he has to be made realize what he is missing. He misses belief in himself or he has very less self-confidence. There is nothing in this world with a fixed date that is known to us. The size judgment we make for a particular task is making us think in that way. He is advised not to measure the size and time, and now he just has to start acting leaving time and size factors.

After few days results had been shared, and he looked satisfied and very happy. He also said that he may not have obtained all the wishes he wished for but he is near to all of them and that too within the very short time which is surprising and unexpected.

From this guy, you can learn very important things for effective planning and its execution and getting success through it. The important things are as follows:

Gain self-confidence as much as possible in the first place before making a plan.

This whole world is filled with too many illusions in which we still live and breaking these illusions is very necessary, and you need to manage them in a right way and start living in real time.

It's our mindset which is really dangerous sometimes. Changing mindset is very necessary for everyone of us, and this change will only bring change in our life. We set limits while making and executing the plans but this is not so true. The end results of any plan cannot be perfect, and there are errors which are always available in our actions.

There is nothing so perfect in this world including your wishes and plans. So don't over think about making perfect plans but just start planning and acting and ignore limited time you have and size of the task from your mind and taking all these rules into consideration will surely help you make and execute plans very effectively.

Productivity secret:

There are no defective plans, and it's the way plan is executed that fails any plan fail, and this happens most of the times.

Effective plans are made by basing one's passion and interest in accomplishing a goal or dream.

16. Get Balanced Mind

"Balanced mindset is a great asset. It helps you have balanced life."

A balanced mind is a very important asset for a productive life. Not many people who even may be successful but don't have a balanced mind. A balanced mind is highly important to have a happy and peaceful life. It is very important to have everything go right in our mind which helps us maintain a healthy mental living for a longer life. It's not money that dictates success or it's not one's authority that dictates success, but it's a balanced lifestyle which dictates success which means having a beautiful and happier life which is full of enthusiasm and energy.

As I told you earlier balanced mind is very necessary to be called as a productive person. To have such balanced mind self-control is very important. Self-control is only possible when you can control things around you in life. The simple way to have great self-control is not allowing your surrounding or situations to affect your mind and this will help you have a balanced mind.

There are several barriers for having a balanced mind. The barriers include laziness, fear, misery, lack of confidence, etc. overcoming these mental barriers is very necessary to have a balanced mind. This world is full of illusions where people work alone with knowledge leaving wisdom, and therefore balanced mind became extinct in this modern world.

So to become human again and to become really productive you need to rejuvenate balanced mind applying principles of ancient wisdom and knowledge.

Humanity restoration can bring back balanced mindset in people of this modern world and let me make it clear for you. There are several organisms on this planet living along with us and what separates us from those creatures is humanity which is about helping and living together. This is the easy way of obtaining balanced mind.

Meditation is one of the processes of obtaining balanced mind, and this had been proved by several great personalities and several types of research. Start the habit of meditation every day. This will help you cleanse your spiritual energy and helps you act normally.

A balanced mind is possible only when hormones that inhibit feelings are in balanced condition. Meditating and taking proper food and having the right amount of sleep helps in having a balanced and healthy mind.

Take any successful men, they have the right amount of sleep, and they take only particular types of foods, and they have very different habits and hobbies when compared to others mostly, and this is what separates them from the rest of the world. Start studying any of the successful people who you may love so much and start learning how they maintain such healthy habits that made them productive and successful.

This will help you learn more about right habits for a balanced mind and also helps you obtain balanced mind in an easy way and takes very little amount of time. There are people who are successful but don't have balanced minds but there are no people who have balanced minds but not successful and act by realizing this point, and it will help you stay wise and productive.

These two good friends helped me find the very importance of balanced life in real life. For convenience let's call them Mr. A and Mr. B and these two guys are very successful, and they have big digit bank balance and they have everything, and they are leading a good life in the society. However, a difference is spotted between those two guys. Mr. A is not as happy as Mr. B is. He always felt that something is missing in his life. But Mr. B is always happy, and he never felt any scarcity.

Mr. A was always worried about obtaining more money, fame and status and he spent very less time with the family which resulted in imbalanced mind, and he never stayed calm and peaceful, but Mr. B is very different to Mr. A.

When Mr. B was enquired about it, He answered that being happy and successful are secondary things in his life and he told that the primary things in his life are his family, relations and people whose presence around him makes his life beautiful and peaceful. He added that this modern world thinks that the big bank balance with many figures brings us everything which is not at all true.

They are after all just figures nothing else. These figures vanish and appear but whereas family and relations are not like it. They always stay with you, inspires you to accomplish anything, appreciates you on success, helps in solving the problem, etc.

There is no need to follow any special methods to have peaceful mind and happiness. You just need to have a happy family where you can understand each other and help each other at all the worst times. You could enhance your happiness by sharing it with people around you. They help you have a balanced mind with ease, and it's the nature way of obtaining happiness and peace.

Many people of the modern world dictate success regarding money and therefore even productivity is measured regarding money which is not so true and incorrect. Productivity shouldn't just produce results, but it should produce everything a life needs. Stop measuring in that way to see the success through the real aperture and start living like a free-minded human. This is the only way you could have a balanced mind by realizing the fact.

Many people ignore the reality of happiness and peace. Only a balanced mind could produce peace and happiness in an individual. To have a happy and peaceful life, you actually need real close people around you who will help you stay hopeful and secure.

Many people ignore their families, relations and acquaintances in hunt of money all their lives which are what they call successful life but at the end of life no money could give you happiness or security that a family can give.

Maintain healthy relationships and give priority to family in comparison to money and this will make you live as a real human being who has balanced the mind. This also helps you really become a productive person.

Keep your life really simple and full of good people, good thoughts and good actions and all these will surely help you gain control over life and construct a balanced mindset without fail.

Productivity secret:

A balanced mind is a very rare asset, and you can get it only by experiencing everything in life.

17. Practice "Best Thinking Habits."

"Best thinking habits help you get success quickly, not easily."

Do you know what the "best thinking habits" are? Have you ever recognized your good habits which are in sync with your sub-conscious mind? Can you answer how these habits are affected by your actions? Answering these questions will help you have a more clear idea of this chapter and helps you use this chapter in a better way in practical life.

Best thinking habits help you to become more concentrated, focused and passionate who ultimately leads to productive life and this leads to success in life. To accomplish any task, you need to have focused the mind and high concentration levels which can only obtain by developing best thinking habits in your life.

Best thinking habits will help you in many ways. They help you have control over your thoughts, concentrate more for longer periods, have a balanced mind, become more productive and successful. These best thinking habits are easy to develop only when you have a clear mind which is free from stress, confusion, and illusions.

There are several best thinking habits you need to develop to attain a stable and peaceful life. However, to become productive, there are certain best thinking habits you can develop and enjoy their outcomes. The best thinking habits to become more productive are in 9 in number are as follows:

A. Think slow, less and act fast.

Thinking is a process which is very random. Thinking process happens faster and slower and at a moderate rate too. These thoughts are decision makers, and they are considered very important while making any final conclusions about anything we do or accomplish. Develop the habit of thinking slowly and clearly without any hurry and act as fast as possible without further thinking about the outcome. This type of thinking habit helps you have control over every situation and helps you grow faster and become productive.

Have a look at successful personalities, and you will find this habit which is why they are really good at having control over things, and they have peace of mind by taking right decisions most of the time.

B. Think independently.

This thinking habit is a very important habit to be developed by many people of the modern world. Developing this habit helps you become action oriented and successful. Many people of the modern world take advice all the time, and they purely depend on other advice without thinking on their own which makes them loose several things in their life.

These people cannot pursue any passions that can make them famous and great. Even ideas which are great are not put into work due to advice from other people. This is due to fear of taking risks and failures. Many people advice not to take any risks to settle well soon, which is very false. They tell you how to run away from risk rather than facing a risk which would bring us success.

What disaster happens when you can't develop this habit can be known from this story of this guy who had failed due to lack of the habit of thinking independently.

People mostly depend on other advice and suggestions to do any work even though they have their own will and guts to pursue their dreams. This type of behavior resulted in the habit of dependence on others even for decisions. This is so true and painful that a human is unable to think clearly and take right decisions on his or her own. Human started acting like robots that have no clear or self-thought making habit. Think independently and take decisions on your own from right now and never think about failures which may or may not occur in future. Live in the present with your own thinking and take any decision on your own. Your decisions may go wrong, but soon you will learn to make proper decisions.

This guy's story moved me and forced me to share this. He is a normal guy like most of the people who are dependent on another point of views. He had a job which paid him well, and he had an idea which could make his life great and could power the other people lives and power the economy.

He wants to work on his idea and make a huge success out of it. He decided to take some advice from his acquaintances and relations. Most of them advised him not to take a risk and do his current job which is paying him well enough. He thought that their advice is right and quit his idea execution plan. His life is just like a clockwork doll running routinely. He had an unsatisfied life which had nothing interesting to him.

One fine day this guy had seen news about another guy who is called as the successful entrepreneur with an idea. The idea that made the entrepreneur so successful is the idea the guy who read news had before, which he quit from execution with the advice of his friends and relations.

On looking at the news, he thought himself that he was the one who has to be in the news but his dependence on others made him lose such great accomplishment which made him feel very sad. He literally cried so much inside and felt very bad for himself for his reliability nature on others.

What made this guy a failure is, his inability to think independently. This kind of habit had brought failures to several people including some of you people who are reading this. This brings us so much pain and loss. Start thinking independently and take right decisions at the right time and this will surely help you win every time.

C. Think like a pro

The power of thinking is unlimited and very surprising sometimes. The power of your thinking could guide you sometimes and sometimes it could even misguide you. The important thing is to become aware of where your thinking is leading you to. What you think is what you become. Your thoughts make you what you think about you. Your thinking has no limits, it can make you anything.

It could make you an animal or mad and there is no limit for thinking process. There is such power to your thinking. Think yourself as a fool all the time, and you would become a fool ultimately. Think yourself as an intelligent, and you would become one someday. Think yourself great sportsmen and you would become one and your thoughts will force you to pursue whatever you think you would be someday. Never think like amateur or newbie while working and thinking so will limit your skills and learning power to low levels and breaking this habit will help you learn and grow faster and you would become a professional at something soon after realizing your thinking power. Always think like professional at work you are doing, and this will help you finish works faster effectively.

This is an example of "you become what you think you are." Therefore think like a pro. This is the story which I had heard when I was a kid. This simple story has a little inspiration for the modern world. There is a guy who is called as a fool by his foes all the time in a school. Gradually this guy turned fool believing what foes called him is true, and even the teacher could not make him brilliant with his teachings and one day this guy who is called as a fool is instructed to leave the school for his no attention in learning.

This guy doesn't know what to tell his father. He started out to his home and in the middle of his way he decided to take some rest. He sat near a well and starting taking rest, and he found a pattern formation near well which is formed due to the placing of water filling vessels at that particular place for filling water.

He realized that the shape or pattern is formed due to the placing of vessels continuously and due to continuous friction between the stone and vessel made the shape or pattern formation possible. Then he realized that he is not a fool and can learn anything with continuous efforts and concentration. He decides to get back to his teacher and ask for one last chance, and he had been given that chance finally.

From that he started learning effectively and continuously using his full concentration and in no time he learned so much and able to succeed than anyone in the school, and from that time no one in the school called him as a fool. This story is simple and cute but has a great message to the world.

Never estimate low about yourself by following others words. You are not less than anyone. You have everything you needed, but you have to realize it. The thought of believing as an intelligent too gave the guy power to excel at learning. Anyone who realizes the talents can surely excel someday.

Many people of his modern world have to understand that, "we are what we think, we are and "we are not what we think, we are not". It's all in our head to excel or loses. Start thinking as professional at any work you do, and you could complete it on time, and this will make you very productive.

D. Think without limits

Limits will limit you from getting success, and they limit you in accomplishing tasks and make you taste failures most of the time. They are considered to be evil unless you have control over them. These limits are eviler when it comes to thinking process. Thinking with limits is considered as limited thinking which always brings you less success. People limit themselves everyday thinking.

The limited thinking thoughts include like I am not beautiful. I am not so much intelligent. I can't earn that much. I can't become rich soon. I am not gifted with any talent. I have no learning skills. I have a problem with communication. I can't accomplish that, I can't get that even if I whole my life, etc. and this list goes on very big. These types of negative thoughts in your brain bring negative results and limit your success to low levels, and this is not correct because no one wants to be a failure.

This particular type of limited thinking is the reason why not all get succeeded and reach their destiny that has been made and stored somewhere in them. This is the cause of failures and the reason why many people live unsatisfied lives. These people never take risks with such limited thinking and fear of failure induced in them with the limited thinking.

Stop limiting your thinking power and keep no limits from now in your life when it mainly comes to success. Think without limits and succeed without limits which make you live a satisfied and happy life soon. Inducing unlimited thinking habit helps you become productive at whatever you do.

In a storybook when I was a child, read this following story which inspired me not to limit my thinking process. In the story, there is a little girl and a hen, who have grown up together and the hen is very big in size as it is well fed from its chicken stage. It's very heavy to lift for anyone but the girl used to lift it easily without any strain because the girl had the habit of lifting it right from her childhood and no one could lift it easily like a girl.

One day the girl is being told that the hen is heavier in weight. It's not easy to lift up and the girl started thinking about the weight of hen is so much. The next day she tried to lift the hen, but she could not live it easily and felt so much strain, and she didn't understand what had happened, and she thought that the hen has gained more weight than before and she just ignored about lifting it again.

The hen actually didn't gain any weight at all. The limited thinking which got developed in girl mind made her think that that way and so she failed at lifting the hen. This story has a lot to teach for the modern world. Many people of modern world limit themselves with the thinking that they can't do few things and eventually they couldn't do them. This makes people unproductive and fails at accomplishing tasks.

Prevention of this limited thinking habit helps you to become productive as you can do anything easily using your full energy and will power.

E. Think flexibly

Flexibility is very important when it comes to thinking. Thinking is a process which can produce thoughts but thinking right and wrong produce two types of thoughts. Thinking in a right way can be considered as thinking flexibly. This thinking is based on the use of wisdom in thinking. Wisdom in us can solve several problems and using it will help you win most of the situations of life. Therefore thinking flexibly helps in solving problems and accomplishing tasks easily. We people have the habit of judging people instantly, and this is the usual way everyone judges the world. Judging instantly will make your judgments go wrong, and this will spoil the relationships between people. Therefore think flexibly and believe that looks don't speak anything about the people and it's very important that consider everyone important and try to understand others. There modify your thinking habit while judging people to have good judgments.

When it comes to becoming productive, many people quit thinking wrong and giving false judgments about their work they have to accomplish. Many people quit from accomplishing works because of false opinions they have to grow in them about work. These opinions act as super barriers for productivity and growing these false opinions over work makes us completely unproductive and lazy at accomplishing things.

Many people suffer from these super barriers which make them fail everyday life. Failure in thinking flexibly results in even a small task looks so much difficult and unimportant. Thinking flexibly helps in getting refrained from this type of false thinking which is making us unproductive. Always look at the work in a right way. Always use your peak energy levels and enthusiasm when doing work and this will help you have more control and right mindset over work. This will help you finish tasks faster at ease.

The effect of non-flexible thinking can be explained with the chain below:

Inflexible thinking→failure in accomplishing tasks→continuous failures→results in laziness

Non-flexible thinking fails you in accomplishing goals or tasks or dreams which result in failures. The continuous failures will result in laziness and procrastination habits in an individual.

F. Think different

Think differently. It doesn't mean you have to think negative or think the reverse. It means think weird, creative, and innovative. Thinking has lot of influence differently in our life. Thinking differently enhances our interest in living and life. You will never feel bored. You will never stay lazy. This type of thinking is very important to stay active all the time.

Do you know? That many innovative people and organizations adopt this habit to become unique and stand out from others. People with habit can be considered as influencers, creators and rule makers. The very powerful leaders have this habit. This habit has no limits, and this works great all the time. Start developing this type of thinking in you to have real control over you and the world.

You can use this type of thinking at your work, and then your work becomes interesting and seems easy to do, and this will help you accomplish tasks faster, and this is the sign of becoming productive.

Never be same as everyone does, and this will help you stand out from the crowd and makes you very successful and the happiest guy.

G. Think positive

Thinking positive is a very powerful habit which not only has got influence over your productive life but also in your personal life. Thinking positive has many benefits. This type of thinking habit helps you make right decisions, and also it helps in thinking right all the time. This type of thinking helps you become an optimist and helps you good in everything which is very necessary for happy and peaceful life.

The power of thinking positive is being explained by several philosophers, successful people, healers, and influencers. They know the true power of being positive in life. People who have positive mind have no failures, and they just have valuable lessons and experiences in their lives. Thinking positive is all about looking at things in a right way. This will automatically grow thinking positive habit in you.

H. Think logically

Logic is the basis for all the decisions we make. It is the basis for thinking we do every day. Every human tries to use his or her logical skills to make right judgments and decisions. Logical thinking has very important place in our brain. Whatever belief we make is as a result of logical analysis.

Without logical thinking habit, a human would become equal to an animal. Logical thinking is what separates human from other species. However, many of us fail to think logically due to illusions ruling us. Break illusions and make your mind very clear and this will help you think logically and help you make right decisions.

Logical thinking is based on pure experiences and situations we have pursued at some point in life. Therefore learn as much as possible to gain more logical skills and access the right things in life. During logical work, skills help you have control over work, and also you will never get bored once you can access your logic for your work and this will make you productive.

I. Think out of box

Think out of the box is not just a habit but an important rule for the modern world. Thinking inside a box makes you lose control over life. Many people live staying inside the box thinking that it is the only world that exists. This will make people live in illusions and have very limited or no success in their lives. They always stay in the box like frogs in a well thinking about the small world they are living in.

Many people in the modern world limit themselves and judge themselves, so basic, and this makes them lose confidence and live like frogs in well forever. They will never know the importance of life. Many of the people are living inside the box and once they start realizing the power if thinking outside the box they will start having real success in their life. Start now realizing that you are not born to live like a frog in the well and come out and see the real world and have right success for yourself.

Many people of the modern world stick to rules and regulations of their work, and this makes people hate their work. Therefore think out of the box from now to explore the wide range possibilities and your capabilities.

Productivity secret:

There are several best thinking habits you could develop and some of the best thinking habits to become productive are 9 and are explained above.

Always think independently and rely on yourself.

Think as professional all the way during your work.

Never judge anything at work to be productive.

18. Improve Every Day and Evaluate

"Success is about improving every day."

Improvement is a natural phenomenon which has its existence in nature. Improvement is very necessary to become more productive and get the success you have dreamt of. Everything gets improved everyday and human too. The improvement that happens to human is based on actions he/she makes every day. There is no human who doesn't want to improve unless he or she doesn't want to succeed.

Improvement is what measures our growth accurately. Improving every day helps you grow faster and get succeed sooner. You need to improve yourself every day to live an amazing life. Improving yourself is easy, and this will make you passionate, enthusiastic and productive. Many people try to improve themselves every day by several ways.

There are several ways you could improve you and become productive. If you want to get improved at work, learn all possible methods and ways to excel at the work you do. Learn from other people who are experts in your field. Learn all possible methods available and make use of them and this way of learning will help you improve faster and become successful with your work.

Artists, authors, writers, businessmen and women, doctors, clerks, professionals, etc. whoever they may be they always try to get improved every day, and so success happens in the process at the end. This is well-known fact to everyone. But not everyone tries to improve their lives.

This 21-day self-improvement and evaluation program helps you improve and work better. This program helps you to improve yourself in any field you wish. This program is not limited to any particular group. During this 21 day program, you have to perform certain tasks to improve yourself. It is as follows.

Day 1: Plan it.

On day 1, you need to make a plan to improve over something. Whatever it may be, it may be at your work, singing, dancing, operating a computer, cooking, cleaning, etc. write down what you have to improve in your life which helps you grow faster and have satisfied living.

Write down only one thing you want to improve. Now write down the ideas of how you want to improve yourself? Write every way you think would be efficient to improve you at something you wished to be good at.

Now filter the ways or methods you have written, and you will come up with very less or few solutions which you think would be effective.

During this phase, you can come up with solutions by researching the ideas and people who are experts at the particular thing you want to improve at. You will find inspiration as well as ideas for improving at something you want.

Write down barriers that are preventing you from improving at something. Evaluate the whole plan again and correct if you find anything odd in the plan.

Day 2: Get ready

Now your planning is over. It's time you should get ready to improve yourself. We have written whatever we need to be considered during the planning phase. Now get ready by making all adjustments you should do. It's not just physical adjustments but mental adjustments too. After strong determination to improve look at the plan all the day and make any possible adjustments.

Write down all the steps you need to pursue to improve yourself. Evaluate all the steps carefully and make any adjustments if necessary.

Day 3-9: Basic execution phase

During this week time executes your ideas and ways to improve you at a basic level. For example, you want to improve your study skills, start reading only for 15 minutes a day with full concentration and efforts. If you want to learn singing, try to learn basics of singing, etc.

During the basic execution phase, you have to excel at fundamentals of something you need to improve at. Learn all basic tips and concentrate more on improvement. This week period can be called as fundamentals improvement phase.

Day 10-14: Medium level phase

As the name suggests you are now well versed with the fundamentals and you can move on with learning basic skills of something you want to improve at.

Start using your basic skills and evaluate the improvement you have made by writing down your feedback regarding the rating.

Now learn all necessary skills in this phase which allows you to enter pro-phase where you are improved at something.

Day 15-20: The pro-phase

During this period you are intermediate, and it's time to bring out your skills at an intermediate level to high professional level. Use all skills you have gained at the medium phase and evaluate the difference between basic and medium level. Now it turns to change your mindset to pro level and think like a pro and learn all necessary skills required and put into practice.

After this time period, you may not be a perfect pro at something, but you will have improved yourself at something you wished to be good at. This method can also be used to learn new skills at ease.

Day 21: Evaluation phase

In this phase challenge yourself. Take any project related to the field you have wished to improve at. Start working on the project and try to complete it as soon as possible and evaluate yourself about your improvement on that particular field by evaluating the project. This way of plan helps you measure the measurement levels and help you gain more success easily. Measuring your improvement levels help you gain more confidence and interest. This also helps in gaining inspiration which helps you excel at things easily.

Every task cannot follow this plan as it has been given a limited time, but this program is not to make you a pro at something. It is being provided to improve you, and when this improvement program is followed for a longer period of time, soon you will become a professional.

Many people have improved themselves using this self-improvement program, and they started loving their work, and also they started finishing tasks faster at ease. This simple 21-day program has a wide range of capabilities when put into real time use.

Improvement is necessary in every field. Improve yourself at managing time for right things, and then you will be called as productive. There are several ways to improve yourself and make sure you are ready to improve and get success.

You are what you do and think, and most important thing is you are what you get improved every day. Your improvement decided who you are? Improvement is the basis for successful life. People who are successful now have not got success just at once. They have improved things in their life every day and made success possible in their life, and they stood out from the crowd and became influencers. To improve you, self-control is a very important aspect, and the way to gain self-control is already explained in the above chapters.

These tasks make you improve your life every day and also make you very productive.

A. Learn a new skill every day or every month or every year.

Certain skills take less time and some skills gaining require more time and learn something new all the time, and this will help you have an idea about every aspect and control over every skill. Doing so will make you multi-skilled which helps you become productive easily.

B. Learn a trick that acts as a catalyst for your work.

Many subjects have some tricks and tips which help us in finishing tasks faster and effectively. Learn all the possible tips and tricks which improve your performance at work you do.

C. Develop passion for the subject

Having passion in life and working will help you perform work with full interest and concentration. This helps in doing your work with whole heart, and this will help you finish tasks faster. Passion drives human mind outside the limits and makes impossible possible which is why developing passion is very necessary to become productive and successful.

Productivity secret:

Learn a skill every day related to your work

Learn a new skill every day which may be you are passionate about.

Learn to evaluate you to find development

PART TWO

19. Reconstructing or Build New Pathways of Processes

"Challenge status quo while planning and this helps you find quick ways to excel."

Any work it may be, it always has pathways or a step-wise process to reach the end. Few tasks have small steps or pathways, and few other tasks have many steps or pathways. This chapter will give you clear idea of reconstructing pathways of a process and make them more effective so that they can be finished so fast which helps you become more productive.

Reconstructing pathways is not an easy task because you need to break your inner mind limits and think again while creating new improved methods or processes for accomplishing tasks. Literally, you have challenge status quo and make better idea and methods work like a charm for any work.

Reconstructing pathways just change the steps of a process but also it changes the entire process of a task to get effective results. Sometimes it could be about bringing in new methods to work and produce best results possible. This reconstruction of pathways is done when you want to minimize the time a work actually takes to complete or if a task produces more errors in practical.

The real magic happens while you are reconstructing a process. During reconstructing a process, it happens that our brain starts brainstorming for new ideas and thoughts and sometimes this lead to building effective processes and sometimes this result in new and innovative discoveries and inventions. While trying to reconstruct a process or build a new process of accomplishing something.

You may come up with numerous ideas and thoughts which are very random, and you try to put them to have the right idea of output we will gain from a particular process. Meanwhile, in the process of reconstruction, it happens that you come up with new discoveries that help you finish tasks faster than you have thought.

Sometimes inventions happen in the process of reconstruction, and many inventions in our modern world are based on this reconstruction principle. Whatever minute invention it may be, it all happened in the process of thinking of reconstructing the processes. Try this rule always, and you will find the real value of it in your practical life.

Take any example starting from cleaning to exploring space. We, human, have created evolved methods which reduced human efforts and time consumption. We have transformed the processes to make it easy for us to finish tasks.

Let's take an example of cutting vegetables. This process of cutting vegetables with the knife used to consume a lot of time and efforts, but in the modern world, it's just matter of very less time, and this process requires fewer efforts with the advent of new methods and inventions which we are using at present. Whatever process it may be evolution has happened slowly and now very new, and easy methods have been made and put into use.

Reconstructing pathways may not bring desired results right away, but they will surely help you become more productive at work you do. They also help you grow enthusiasm and innovation in you. Sometimes reconstructing pathways require more time, and this could be considered as wasted time if proper solutions are not found but never treat it as lost time because you have come up with all possibilities and impossibilities of a process which makes you a professional at that particular process. At least you have gained exquisite knowledge at something you are working at, and this will help you grow interested, in the particular work.

Artists, businessmen, scientists, professionals, and teachers, etc. use this reconstruction method to bring out more results. Whoever it may be if they want to improve they have to modify and optimize the existed things to get increased outcome from their efforts. There are several ways of reconstructing pathways for a process, and every method has its own importance. Even this reconstruction of pathways is used in scientific development processes. This principle has a lot of importance, and one who knows it will surely get the success they have always desired.

This one method has shown the improved results which are actually used in the reconstruction of a process. The method can be understood as follows in a stepwise manner.

Step 1: write it down

Write down the process in a stepwise manner on paper. In this step write every possible step you are taking to complete a task and make sure every step is recorded on the paper.

Step 2: Assessment phase

This is most crucial and important step one has to pursue. In this step evaluation of all steps has to be done carefully and make sure everything is okay. Understand every step clearly.

Step 3: priority factor rule

In this step, the priority rule comes into action. According to this rule, important steps have to be considered, and these steps have to be separated from the list and make a new list in which only new steps have been recorded.

Step 4: Optimization rule

Now from the important steps optimize the steps if possible to bring out more desired results. This optimization helps you minimize the effects of removal of unimportant steps of a process.

Step 5: pack up rule

This is the final step in which you have to finish reconstructing the rule. Before finalizing make sure everything is good and continues to the execution phase which also can be considered as a trial period in which we get results of our reconstructed process. If the process you have constructed gave you desired results, then congrats on your first improvement trial. You can use this method all the time to improve your productive life.

Productivity secret:

Always minimize the number of steps in a process.

Take one big step or several steps to improve or reinvent a process or pathway.

20. Developing Accuracy and Speed

"Accuracy and Speed are factors which dictate success."

Accuracy and speed are great enemies most of the times. They hate each other, and that is why they do not co-exist most of the times. These best enemies result in human failures and let me explain you this clearly. In this modern world speed dictates, productivity and accuracy fail to show its part in productive life. They are part of every work we do or perform.

The task or process which uses accuracy cannot be accomplished at speed, and the task or process which uses speed cannot be performed accurately. These are two conditions which make work unsatisfactory which misses either accuracy or speed factors. This makes us unproductive at many times. There is very equal importance for both speed and accuracy. When you can have speed and accuracy with your work, you can excel at the work you do.

Making speed and accuracy co-exist is the difficult task for many of us. There are several ways which can complete a work accurately but consumes lot of time, and here speed is the missing factor. There are several ways which can complete a task at great speed, but accuracy factor will be missing here. If any of the factors from speed and accuracy are missing, then it is considered as an unproductive way of doing that particular task.

Developing these speed and accuracy factors is very important to become really productive. These factors decide your success and productive life. Therefore it is very important to concentrate on these two factors for a productive life.

These two important factors, speed and accuracy have an origin in you, and therefore these two important points should be considered.

A. When speed and accuracy are best enemies, you will always face failure in life.
B. When speed and accuracy are best friends, you will always find success in life.

The two above points could teach you a lot. It's up to you to decide which one is better for you. When you create strong bondage between speed in your mind, and it happens that you will fall in love with the thing you want to excel someday and it becomes your passion.

When the above becomes possible, speed and accuracy becomes great friends and helps you win every time you act. This way you could bond speed and accuracy and make them your friends.

Many people want to excel at something. Speed and accuracy factors help you become excel at that thing you want. Therefore developing speed and accuracy in work is very important. This is only possibly by loving the work you do or do the work you love.

Remove your mental barriers on anything you do, and this will surely help you bring out your speed and accuracy that can dictate your success and productivity life. Many people who are very successful know this principle consciously or sub-consciously which made them very successful and making them successful.

Productivity secret:

To make accuracy and speed, stay together while working or performing a task, love the work you do or grow interest, in work you do.

You can improve your interest in work by learning new skills and tricks which help you accomplish your work faster and in an effective way.

21. TRANSFORM TRAVEL TIME TO PRODUCTIVE TIME

"Use time in a wise way, you have got it very less."

Who doesn't love traveling? Everyone does or most of us do. Travelling is really fun, and traveling helps you learn several things, and you will get several experiences which you will miss if you don't travel. There are several people who know real benefits of traveling, and they always love traveling to different places. Such very good time can be used for productivity. When you enjoy the journey, keep enjoying but if it's boring just transform into productive time.

Write something while traveling or read a book or you could attend a webinar that teaches you a new skill, or you could draw a picture or anything else that is considered as a productive task.

If you are a regular traveler, this principle is really very helpful to you. It's very important that time should not be wasted just like that as it is more precious and cannot be brought back what efforts you may put. Therefore you must use your available time while traveling for something else which makes you productive.

One of my personal experiences taught me the importance of using this principle. While traveling on tour, I started using this principle, and this all happened suddenly. I was traveling on tour with my friends and colleagues, and this tour seemed boring. Even though I am not alone, I felt like I am alone because of addiction of people to technology.

Most time people in journey has spent their time on their technology gadgets like mobiles, laptops, etc. rather than talking to people, having fun, etc. which is, of course, most commonly happening thing for many of us in the modern world. I like traveling and this journey was boring. I felt that It would have been a more great journey if I had traveled it alone and this was the feeling I got watching everyone around me.

I decided to do something that will prevent me getting bored and so I usually carry my bag which has a book and pen. I took out my book and started writing something on the first day. I scribbled several ideas and thoughts in the book. It was 10 days trip, and I have to make it more awesome by some way.

Then I decided to write stories by taking any events I see around me while traveling and I started doing it from the second day. I noted everything I felt important I saw. Then I joined the things that I saw and started making short stories, and finally, at the end of the day I have written few stories, and altogether I have written a book which had a collection of stories which will be published soon.

Even though I could not enjoy the journey, I have my own satisfaction that I had learned something from that long journey. I learned to observe things, and I learned to make my writing better, and I became very good at analyzing things, and this all together made me feel very productive at the end of the day. From that day I started using the principle without fail for enhancing my productive life, and you could do it too if you use this principle in practical life to become productive.

Always remember to use the time in some way. Never sit idle because time is more precious and valuable asset which can never be gained back once you lost it on nothing.

Productivity secret:

Carry a log book and a pen whenever you travel because thoughts flow just like your journey.

Listen to an audio book or podcast while traveling.

22. Organize Workspace

"Best environment helps you concentrate more and makes you productive."

A well-organized workspace could save you so much time, and this helps you become productive too. Many people ignore about organizing their workspace, and they spend very much time wasting on searching for important things such as files, stationery, etc. in their workplace. This time which is wasted in searching could be used for accomplishing some other tasks that make you productive. The unorganized workspace will make you lose so much time, and even your mind goes unorganized.

The unorganized workspace can cause several problems which will make you unproductive and stressful. The biggest problems you could face due to the disorganized workspace is you will become a long-term searcher for needed things or objects. You won't find what you need in a chaotic space, and this result in stress and loss. Sometimes you spend money buying objects and information you need as you didn't find them when they are needed. This results in loss of time, money and mental peace which makes you unproductive.

We can't remember things we placed in an unorganized workspace, and this will result in severe problems. You may start hating your work due to the unorganized workspace which makes you unproductive at work. A good environment is very important for working and disorganized space converts a good environment into an unproductive environment which effects productive life.

Follow these little steps to have an organized workspace and organized mind:

Remember to maintain a simple workspace where you feel inspired all the way doing your work. Maintain particular way of holding things such as files, stationery, etc. to save time and have stress free life.

Decorate your workspace in a way that always inspires you to work and in an experiment we have proved that getting inspired and working makes you work more efficiently and make you very productive. Try to find inspiration in your workplace to find you work interesting.

Place anything away that distracts you in the workspace, and this will help you get away from distractions and become productive at work.

The technology of modern world distracts very much our work which should be avoided. You could maintain separate room for your tech gadgets and workspace, or you could divide your room in half and place your workspace on one side and tech gadgets such as your Pc or Mac and mobiles on another side. This will help you refrain from getting distracted by technology devices and helps you concentrate on your work alone for a longer time. This little tip could mainly help artists, writers, authors and anyone who do creative work.

Maintain separate folder space just like you use on your Pc or Mac or Mobile in your workspace and place a particular type of documents in that space which will help you have organized space that helps you find whatever you want when you need at ease.

We know that physical things have greater influence over our mind and therefore it is very important to maintain physical things in a good manner in the workspace. Decorate your workspace in the way you love. Make your workspace look simple and modern. Place posters, vision charts which inspire you. Fill the room with a fragrance you love and place native flowers that you love and change them every day. This helps you have full energy while working in the workspace as it is in the way you love.

Make your workspace free from interruptions and distractions by making all possible changes you need to make.

Allow natural light to pass into your workspace, and this will help you live and work in a day style. Natural light has a greater influence on our body and brain, and this can make you really productive at work you do.

Everything in your workspace should be perfect for you. This may include tiny things such as the size of the room, a pleasant color painted in the room, furniture arrangement, etc. your working environment has its direct impact on work you do and therefore it is very necessary to maintain proper environment.

Arrange everything in a particular way that makes it easy for you to get whatever you want just in time. This will save you lot of time and efforts.

Place an alarm clock or timer in your room and set strong end points for tasks you have to complete.

Stick a poster on the wall in which your biggest passion or dream to be accomplished is written on it along with a deadline and continue to do this for your every dream you want to bring to life.

Place unnecessary stuff like unnecessary files, technology devices or anything that distracts you away from the room for a peaceful environment which helps you work more efficiently.

There is tremendous importance for workspace as our whole way of working purely depends on the workplace. Maintaining a favorable environment for work is crucial and therefore organizing your workspace is necessary. Several prominent and successful companies follow the principle of organizing workspace in their offices as they always wish to be successful and productive.

This way of organizing the workspace and maintain good work environment is one of the success secrets for every successful company, and this is also the one of the success principles of individuals who is passionate and successful.

For a change, we have interviewed small businesses which are not growing at all about their workspace to find out whether there is any effect due to the unorganized workspace. Our team has approached the small businesses and started interviewing.

The results are really surprising, but they are what we have expected to find out. Many owners of small businesses stated that they don't have a perfect organized workspace. They added that they have several barriers that are not allowing their business growth. When asked about the conditions of their workspace, they narrated the whole environment in their workspace, and there are several blunders in the work environment which made them work under unproductive conditions.

We had made some changes in the work environment and waited for improved results. There was no natural light falling into the workplace, and there is no proper light, and the workspace is fully messy. We had suggested few changes in the workspace like there should natural light getting in and therefore the natural light emitting bulbs are installed, and they were advised to clean the room completely and arrange things properly. The walls were filled with inspirational posters. Flowers are placed in the corners, and they should be changed every day. These things have to be continued for a week, and then feedback is taken from the employees of the office.

After a week the owner of that small business approached us and spoke in a happy way that he had seen his employees working more efficient than before. He also added that there was more interest and enthusiasm in work shown by employees in that week. He never cared about changing the workspace but from the day he started changes and improvement he began believing in every small thing which helped him build confidence.

This small experiment by us brought desired results and proved the efficiency of organizing workspace in becoming productive at work. A good workspace acts as an excellent factor for quality of work life. It should be realized that physical workspace has direct influence over work we do.

In the process of experiment, we have created two types of environments from which the efficiency of work done is calculated. The two categories of environments are as follows explained below:

A. Open type workspace environment

In this environment space is arranged in a way that looks natural and beautiful. There are natural light, flowers and symmetric arrangement of things in the room which include furniture, stationery, etc. then a group of volunteers is allowed to work in that environment.

B. Closed type workspace environment

In this environment, there is no natural light and this environment looks artificial and beautiful but there is no possibility of exposure of volunteers who will work in this environment to external natural environment, and then the group of workers is allowed to work in this environment.

From above two types of environment, the results are noted, and the differences are calculated and analyzed. The feedback of how volunteers felt in both the environments is also taken into consideration.

It has been found that people who worked in open type workspace environment showed high energy levels at work, and also they showed productive results than people who worked in the closed type workspace environment. It is found that people work more efficiently when they are exposed to the natural environment than closed environments.

The energy levels of people in open type environment are higher than in closed type environment. The people in the free environment also showed their joy and interest in working whereas people in closed environment seemed dull and their faces didn't express the joy of working or their high energy levels.

This one experiment proved the importance of well organized open type workspace which results in high productivity levels. Always try to maintain work environments which will help you become creative and productive at work.

In the end, we asked for a genuine feedback from theses volunteers, and it is found that volunteers in open type workspace environment are highly motivated to work naturally and showed high satisfaction levels whereas feedback is less in comparison in case of volunteers who worked in closed environments.

Always create a proper workspace to become more efficient at the work you do. This helps you become not only productive but also helps you gain mental peace at work and brings down your stress levels and allows you to work effectively.

Productivity secret:

The best working environment is a very necessary aspect to become productive.

Clean workspace helps you have a peaceful mind.

23. Creating Action Posters

"Action posters help you act more to finish accomplishing your dreams and goals."

This is one most important method to become highly motivated to work and become productive. Action posters are the posters which contain information regarding your dreams, actions, passions and deadlines in which you have to accomplish things in your life. These posters are attached to your wall or workplace where your sight usually goes.

Action posters are individual charts which keep your dreams and passion alive and make them more rememberable most of the time. Action charts are simple to make, and they have very effective influence in making you productive. These posters are highly important as they motivate you to concentrate on your dreams, passions, and things you have to accomplish in your life.

This is a story of a guy who inspired himself to accomplish his works using Action posters. He shared his story of how those action posters influenced him to work more on his dreams. He said that he lose interest in his work so much fast and it takes a lot of time to regain his interest to work again. This made him unproductive at work he does and gradually started living unsatisfied life every day.

He hated his way of living and searched for several solutions and this action posters strategy worked well for him. He said that he made a poster which is filled with a single big task he has to accomplish in his life and a deadline is provided too, in the poster, and this poster is attached to the wall where he usually had his sight.

Every day when he gets up he could see his biggest dream to accomplish and seeing this he is motivated to start doing his work fast and whenever he feels like he is losing interest he see the poster, and this help him to get inspired and work again with full energy. He continued to use this strategy for over extended period of time and accomplished several big dreams he had in his life.

The story of this guy can tell you the importance of posters that inspire us to work every day with full interest to accomplish our goals, dreams or passions. These posters are your allies who help you concentrate on your goals and dreams.

Many people in this modern world have the problem of losing interest in work very soon, and this is making them unproductive at the work they do. This is becoming a barrier that is preventing people from getting success. People have great ideas, but they are not ready to execute as they lack interest gradually due to postponing the goal to some other day. To keep your inspiration and motivation alive, you need to have a continuous interest in work you do and keep doing the work without stopping.

These action posters can help you get inspired which tells you to work for your goals and accomplish them on time and have success in life. These action posters are your best friends when you do what they say that is what is written by you on them.

These are very simple charts which have massive influence over your work when they are made correctly. The imperative components of good action posters are your dream or goal or passion and a perfect deadline and write your "why?" that is the reason behind accomplishing your dream or goal.

The process of creating action poster is as follows in the stepwise way shown below.

Step1: write or draw the initial point that is where you are now, you can call it the initial stage of your plan to accomplish a goal or dream. This should be at one side of the poster.

Step 2: write or draw the end point that is where you want to be, you can call it the final stage where you have accomplished the goal or dream. This way of writing inspires your subconscious mind to create belief and confidence in your goal or dream or passion. This should be written or drawn on another side and make sure the space between initial and end steps is empty where you are going to plan real things for accomplishing your goals or dreams.

Step 3: now draw a line between the initial step and end step and write down your plan to achieve your goal and reach the end step which is what you have dreamt of to be. Write down "why?" factor which helps you keep inspired.

Step 4: write a deadline in which you could pursue your dream or goal. Write the deadline in big bold letters.

Step 5: now it's time to decorate your poster. Make your poster look straightforward and beautiful to see. This will help you get your attention to the poster every day. Write the initial point and final steps of your action plan in big bold letters that they can be seen even from long distance.

This 5 step plan could help you make the best poster for your goal or dream. Call this poster an action plan for your goal. Vision yourself where you will be after accomplishing the dream or goal. For example, you want to be a singer try to visualize yourself as a singer, and this will help you make a better plan.

Another way of creating action poster is just write down your one big goal you want to work on in big letters and write a deadline and just stick it to the wall to save time designing the posters, and this would be preferred method for simplicity lovers.

This crafting of action poster helps you has great confidence and belief in your dream, passion or goal. Only who wants to become productive accomplishing goals without losing interest can make more out of this creating action poster strategy. Make your poster now start you trials to become very productive at your work with full interest and passion.

Productivity secret:

Action posters help you remember your goals and dreams.

Design action posters in a beautiful way or a simple way.

24. Plan 'it' in advance

> "Planning in advance helps you live and pursue future before it actually happens."

This is one of the best tips to make every day feel motivated and inspired to work very efficiently. How about planning a day in advance? How about living an extra day in peace and joy? How about doing things in right time and right way? All these are possible if you can understand this principle and make use of it in your practical work life.

You could become productive if you make this principle your daily usual habit. Everyone plans and not every plan succeeds. This chapter doesn't teach you the complex way of planning things. It's the way you could use to plan small things every day and accomplish them within the time and have mental peace whole day.

To have a good day every day, you need to do things you desired of doing in time so that you could get the desired results in time. This is the simple strategy which helped people not only get success but also made them very productive. This planning in advance became their habit.

The only thing you need to do is plan in advance what you have to do. It's about planning tomorrow tasks today itself. The tomorrow has to start today itself. What you need to do is plan what you have to do tomorrow has to be planned today itself. The best time to do this is the night before sleep that is before another day appears.

This is not just a plan but a better way to make every tomorrow hopeful which helps you have full energy and concentration over any work you do tomorrow. This strategy helped many people to make success in their life and become productive, and this could help you too. The method of planning this advance to do list for tomorrow is very simple and takes a little practice. The only thing you face as the problem is executing your plan successfully.

For some people, it may look odd of planning tomorrow today itself as they are believers of living in the present. Their way living is right but building future along with living present would give us more success and happiness. The planning in advance can be as follows in a stepwise manner.

Step 1: Initially write down the draft of tasks you have to accomplish for tomorrow. Now filter the list by giving priority to most important tasks and make sure you complete them in time.

Step 2: next now you have a list and arrange all the tasks in an order based on your priority and give some amount of time to each task.

Step 3: now from the organized list, rearrange the task list based on time consumption. Some tasks require more time and efforts and do them first, and therefore they have to be place in the initial phase in the list and the task that consumes less time should be at the end.

Step 4: Finalize the list by checking everything in the list is correct and now go to bed and have sleep.

This is how you could use those steps to build an advance plan list today for living a better tomorrow. Use this way of planning every day and start doing tasks right from the morning. One more tip for better performance would be is do very important tasks in the early morning, and they consume less time and save you more time for other tasks you should accomplish.

This type of advanced planning helps you become prepared for future every day and when this is continuously done, it becomes a habit with which you build not only success but also productive life.

This chain shows how you could make a day hopeful and happy by accomplishing everything you desired of, using the advanced planning strategy or plan in advance strategy.

Advance plan→accomplish tasks→fill happiness and satisfaction→repeat

This planning in advance helps you accomplish tasks effectively, and this will fill your life with happiness and satisfaction.

Being prepared earlier will help you bring down your stress levels and help you become more peaceful and concentrated at the work you do.

This strategy also helps you fill every day full of energy, enthusiasm, and motivation which act as fuels for a productive life.

Start using this strategy to become productive and successful at work, and you could save more time and energy which could be spent on vacation or family which helps you build mental peace and good relationship.

Productivity secret:
> Advance plans help you stay prepared for tomorrow
> Advance planning helps you build a secure future.

25. Act Like an Introvert

"Introverts are more successful and productive and learn their personalities at work."

Do you know how an introvert behavior exists? Do you know the importance of being an introvert at work? Have you ever thought of becoming an introvert? Answering these questions will help you have a good idea about introverts, and this will help you become productive at work and also successful too.

Becoming an introvert at work makes you productive and successful. Introverts spend very less time with the people. They talk less. They are less socializing. They are alone, but they are real influencers.

It has been found that people who are in top positions are introverts and the success is because of the productiveness. Introverts may not be very good at socializing in groups or meetings or group work, but they are really good and sincere at self.

The power of introvert habits has more influence in productivity life. Try to learn introvert habits at work, and this will help you become more productive and successful. This is the new way of becoming productive, and it's a way of getting success through influence over self.

The very important reason why you need to act like an introvert is this. This difference between extroverts and introverts help you to understand why you should act like an introvert.

The following differences realize the very importance of becoming an introvert while working.

1. Extroverts speak a lot and sometimes waste time talking to people leaving the work unfinished. However introverts talk less, and they give priority to their work, goals, and passion, so they never chat without finishing their work in time.
2. Extroverts make their social skills speak for themselves, but introverts make their actions speak about them, and their actions bring fame and success that last longer to remember for people.
3. Introverts have a lot of self-respect for themselves, and this self-esteem makes them do activities that reflect their influence and power to the

world. Extroverts may not have such self-respect the introverts have as they always compromise with themselves and people.

4. Introverts spend their leisure time reading a book which is his/her best friend. Extroverts spend time with people through meetings, chatting, etc. introverts are considered productive as their habit of reading helps them learn something however extroverts waste time by spending leisure time on unnecessary talks and meetings.
5. Extroverts work for others which are to impress others and get into notice, and this makes them unproductive whereas introverts work for themselves that is to satisfy themselves by their actions, and they always finish tasks in time and make their work speak for them which is a sign of productive habit.
6. Introverts never feel alone as they will always be busy doing something that makes them excel at the wok. Extroverts feel loneliness whenever they alone don't know what to do.
7. Extroverts work for success and fame, but introverts work for satisfaction and mental peace.
8. Introverts disconnect from the world while working which make them free from distractions and interruptions whereas extroverts stay connected with the world while working and therefore they cannot escape from distractions and interruptions.

The above 8 difference can tell you the importance of being an introvert at work. You will never hate your work, and you will always work to excel at self. Living like an introvert and extrovert both have their own advantages but at work being an introvert has real strong advantages which help you become productive and succeed at your work.

You can understand the power of becoming an introvert at work by studying some big personalities who are scientists, businessmen, artists or authors. Study their habits at work, and this will help you learn more habits of excelling at your work.

Many great personalities who are successful always get disconnected from the work which enables them to concentrate more on their work and find success. This is, of course, the best way to become productive and successful in a new way. You don't need to be an introvert all the time in your life but at work try to become one which helps you excel at your work.

Many individuals who are successful are neither introverts nor extroverts. They are a combination of both, and this enables him to become productive and get success. So don't worry about becoming an introvert forever. You could be both and adjust yourself to anyone based on requirement and priority of work you do.

To find the efficiency of introverts at work, we did a small experiment. In the experiment, we have selected a group of people. Initially, they are given work to do, and after accomplishment, the results are recorded and then they are instructed to act as introverts by studying the above 8 rules and then the experiment has begun. After getting ready by studying the above habits we had told the group of people to act like introverts at work. They were instructed to start working and at the end results are recorded and analyzed by comparing before and after studying 8 habits of introverts.

The results are really amazing and surprising. The results have shown high productivity rate after studying introvert habits and pursuing them while working. This simple experiment gave us the proof of wide possibilities of being an introvert at work. You could use the introvert habits for work and gain productivity and success. Get ready to live like a pro by becoming productive using introvert habits. It's all to you to whether to succeed or fail and the most important thing is to live a peaceful life.

Productivity secret:

Learn to be an introvert at work because they are very less distracted at work.

26. TRY 50/50 RULE

"When it's difficult to understand or pursue, try breaking it into pieces."

This 50/50 rule is very new one which helps you gain the confidence of becoming productive at your work. This rule helps you change your mindset over work. For example, a task seems so hard but when you start using this rule the same task looks easy, and this helps you work better at a task accomplishment.

This rule is very simple and can be put into use very quickly. The rule can be used to divide a task. There is a barrier in our brain that creates fear in us which acts as a real barrier in accomplishing greater or bigger tasks. The thought of bigger or higher creates an illusion of "I may not do it," which will make lose confidence in you and the work you have to accomplish.

This type of thinking leads to failures without any doubt. This type of thinking leads to becoming quitters and not- initiative takers at risks. You will have to live a compromised and unsatisfied life forever. This rule is like, do at least half the whole task or break the task into more small parts which you can do in a better way.

This is how you could make use of 50/50 rule to become conscious and productive at a particular task you do. The rule goes like this. Let's take a task and give a notation 'A' for the task which consumes so much time and efforts. When our brain feels a task as the hard one, our brain starts making so many false conclusions about that particular work such as it takes so much time and it may be risky, and I may fail in accomplishing the task, etc. which most brains start making false assumptions about the work. This results in fear of failure even though we didn't start doing the work which results in not trying the task.

So let's make it easy for our brains using 50/50 rule. Let's break the task 'A' into parts. This breaking of a task into steps is based on time and efforts it takes. Let's take work can be done in two steps in a day. Then make the task into two parts that is 50/50. Therefore there are two steps for this particular work and the day can be divided into two parts, and the two steps have to be done which results in finishing the task. If the task A takes more time and has several steps, then break the step 1 into two sub-steps and go on breaking the task until you feel it as an easy task to accomplish.

This rule makes you feel free to work and therefore taking the initiative becomes easy and possible. Many failures in this world are due to fail in taking action which can be overcome using this 50/50 rule. This way of breaking make you feel every task very easy to perform, how many efforts and time it may take. When you start using this rule every time, it helps you grow big from small. Many people of the modern world have fear at accomplishing big things, but it's time you have to realize that the little things pave the path to big things in life.

Always have faith in you, and this is the only fuel which can run your internal work clock to longer distances and bring you real success and happiness. Never stop doing things if you feel them hard and always try to find a proper solution.

Productivity secret:

> Break a bigger task into several small parts until it feels very easy to start and finish.

27. Use Filtering Method

A day just doesn't have a few tasks to accomplish. There may be numerous tasks you have to do. Even the whole day may not be sufficient to finish all the tasks we have to accomplish. This may result in failure at performing certain important tasks which make you lose the mental peace. This also makes you unproductive at work. This method is mainly made to help you get to refrain from the problems I have mentioned in above lines. This method works like a charm, and this is the easiest method you can ever have in your daily life which helps you finish important tasks on time and have mental peace which ultimately helps you become productive.

The filtering method is a simple, unique method which helps you give an arrangement to your tasks which could be done in a day or a week or a month or a year or in a lifetime. The filtering is based on priority we give to each task in our life.

This method could be used to accomplish your dreams and goals one by one or to accomplish your daily routine tasks and any other tasks you do in your daily life. Whatever it may be the important thing is to you is to believe in the method and yourself. This makes you excel at the work using the method for sure.

The filtering method goes like this in real use. In this method, there are several simple steps you need to follow. This method starts with planning.

1. Plan a list of works you have to do in a day and try to do this one day before at night and more about it check plan in advance section which I have shared with you earlier.
2. Now based on priority filter the list that has numerous tasks you have to accomplish in a day. Now only very important tasks are present in the list and let's call it priority list of tasks.
3. In this step, the priority list of tasks is again filtered based on hard and easy factors. The starting of the list has to start with hard, important tasks first and easy tasks later.
4. In this step separate out tasks that can be done in a matter of just minutes and enter them into another list and now start doing these tasks first and this will enable you to grow confidence while working.

5. In this step start doing hard tasks first and after completing them go for easy tasks. This will help you finish hard tasks first, and so you could have more mental peace and satisfaction.

This 5 step process of filtering, works like a charm when properly put into use. The importance of this method is to make you productive by helping you accomplish important tasks first every day, and this will help you what actually has to finish and what has to just leave in a day. You could use this method for long term goals and the process of planning in same but replace tasks with your goals or dream you have to accomplish in life.

Productivity secret:

Filtering system for tasks or goals or dreams helps you concentrate more on important things.

28. Curing Procrastination

"Procrastination kills productive life and makes you live hell on heaven."

Procrastination is really evil. It makes any human go through a hard phase of life. It results in failures. It results in laziness. It also results in making you stressful and sad all your life. This procrastination is an appalling habit which could never allow you to grow in your life and in turn it could destroy your peaceful living and make you a failure that never has mental happiness all the life.

Therefore knowing the effects of procrastination you need to cure procrastination in you by some way. All the problems that may cause due to procrastination have been shared with you. It's your turn to realize it and make the right decision that is whether to cure procrastination and live a free life or stick to procrastination habits and like nothing. It's up to you who have to make the right decision.

As it is very hard to cure procrastination, we tried to cure it by finding out the causes of procrastination which would give a clear idea of developing ways to cure procrastination. A reverse engineering process is used employed to find out all the possible ways that cause procrastination habit get drawn up in us.

To find out the reasons we have interviewed several people about how they started to procrastinate and what lead them to become lazy. We interviewed about how and why they became procrastinators. This way interviewing gave us surprising reasons for the cause of procrastination. The reasons are really simple, but they are unexpected reasons by us which we found from the interview.

The main causes of procrastination were figured out from the interview and are shared as follows. There are top three reasons for people becoming procrastinators.

1. **Fear of failure**

   This is the number one reason most people reported us as a reason for procrastination. Many people quit from doing things due to fear of failure, and gradually they became procrastinators. The only way to face this fear of failure in us is only possible by doing actions or taking initiatives.

Any task it may be, there are only two outcomes that are it will be either success or failure. But the important thing to understand is you cannot expect results without making trials. Facing the fear of failure is very important to become anti-procrastinators. Fear of failure can only be eradicated by starting taking actions.

You may win or fail, but you will never have to quit which is a very important rule to keep in mind. Not doing anything is not so good than winning or losing and therefore you need to realize that fear is drawing you back and making you lazy and timid which act as barriers to not only your productive life but also affecting tour personal life in every aspect. Only through realizing the evil influence of fear over you helps you fight with it by starting making actions.

Believe me fear cause death every second of life and it's up to you whether to live or die every second of your life. When you realize this and start acting, you will find your success soon and can cure procrastination.

2. **Lack of interest**

    This is the number two reason why people became procrastinators. They are many people in this world who compromise with the things in daily life. This compromising habit, at work, made these people hate their work, and so they ended up becoming procrastinators at work. They actually lost interest in their work as they have compromised with their dreams and passions and doing some routine and tedious work daily. This type of lifestyle leads to laziness in people which made them procrastinators.

    The people became procrastinators as they started compromising with their lifestyle every day just like many of the people in the modern world. It is found in research that about 80% of employees want to change their jobs as they lack interest in the current jobs which would bring the world more procrastinators into life making the world unproductive. Therefore the only way to prevent yourself from becoming procrastinators is to do the work you love from today. Another way would be to love the work you do. Any of these ways would cure procrastination in you. To love the work you do, find why of your work which helps you have the right idea about the work you do and make you whether to love or leave your work.

3. **Trying to be perfect**

    This is the number three reason why people are becoming procrastinators. There is nothing in this world which is perfect which the fact everyone has to realize is. Even nature has its own drawbacks. At work, there is the possibility of perfection at all. There are errors that are common during the process of accomplishing the work. These small or big errors are making people lose their interest in work and in turn making people lose self-confidence which is a real disaster.

Therefore never try to be perfect at work. Try to make things better not perfect, and this will help you gain more and more confidence with the work you do, and as a result, you could accomplish the work at a faster rate and have excellence possible which is what the desired outcome is.

These three top reasons will make anyone become procrastinator very soon. Therefore make your mind be in control before you start becoming a procrastinator. The only way to cure procrastination is to keep you in control and taking actions all the way. This type of behavior will surely help you become anti-procrastinator and also helps you cure procrastination in life. It's your turn to build a strong anti-procrastination shield around you before it's too late. You could follow the prevention of procrastination is better than cure principle over here.

Productivity secret:

> There are several barriers which make to a procrastinator.
> Try avoiding those barriers.

29. STOP WORRYING ABOUT RESULTS

"Results happen at the end and worrying about results ends your productive life at the start."

Results happen from any task you accomplish. They are a common outcome of every task. The most important thing is these results are unpredictable, and they may or may not meet our expectations sometimes. Worrying about them doesn't make any sense at all. Many people make this mistake of worrying about results all the time. They always think of results and gets poor at work they do which make them unproductive at work.

Worrying about results grow stress in your mind which becomes a barrier for accomplishing tasks on time. This lead to loss of confidence at work we do. Instead, you could think of improvement you have made every day at your work which helps you gain more confidence and helps you finish tasks fast.

You could focus on what you have completed than what you have to complete, and this will make you forget about results and keep working. The results which occur at the end are not predictable. They may be more than want we have expected, or they may be less than what we have expected or they may be what we expected. As they are unpredictable, it's better to forget about them and keep working until you get succeed.

This way of not worrying about the results has several advantages. They are as follows:

a. You could have mental peace at work as you are not worried about results.
b. You could be able to gain confidence by measuring the improvement not your results.
c. You will have a freedom mind which can think and make you act more than before.
d. You could measure the self-improvement at work.
e. You could focus on the process rather than results. This is very important for getting more productive.
f. You will love the work rather than hate it.

g. You will become stress-free soon, and this will help you have peace in life.
h. This gives you mental ability to think clearly and make right decisions on time.
i. It gives you freedom to excel at work by finishing them in time or one time at ease.

All these help you have a clear way for working and become more productive. The most important thing to remember is not to think of results. They always happen from your actions some day. Concentrate on how you work and how you act and develop yourself more at your skills and this will help you become very productive.

The only thing it matters is having a balanced, peaceful mind which is very necessary to work effectively and bring out desired results, and this is only possible by not thinking about results. This is the fascinating rule for accomplishing things without quitting.

This chain shows the impact of worrying about results and not worrying about results while performing a task or work.

a. Worrying about results→failure to concentrate on work process→end up quitting or work unfinished
b. Not worrying about results→able to focus on work process→can finish task on time and results are as expected.

The two chains could show the importance of this rule at work in your daily life and make use of it carefully in practical life.

I know a guy who always worries about the results ever time he starts a task. As the work moves on he gradually end up with stress and sometimes he quit his work. This made him lose control over things in his life. The reason is he always wants fast results which are not at all possible before completing the task or work he does. But his thinking about work made him feel the work should be completed very soon. This results must be out, but the tasks take more time period to get finished, and he wants to do them before time which is not possible for him, and this made him lose interest in the work he is doing, and soon he quit his work every time.

But a day has come which made him realize the importance of patience. He decided to be patient for results. He decided not to worry about results anymore. He thought that let a task takes its own time to complete with its own needed deadline. This mental shift in him had made him have mental peace at work from that day. He never thought of results. He always thought of improving the work, and this made him live a free life which gave him the freedom to excel at work.

From that particular day of realization, he was able to complete all task in time or before time which showed the signs of productiveness. He is able to have mental peace and make right decisions at the right time which helped him win at many situations in his life. All these things had become possible only by this simple trick of not thinking about the results.

Many people just like the guy above have the habit of thinking about results, and there are not worried about starting the work or doing the work effectively but interested in only results, which is very wrong. Instead of worrying about results start worrying about working efficiently, and this will bring you good results for sure.

The results are the outcome of what we do and how we do things. They are the outcome from us. They are controllable only if you could work effectively. Therefore have a right mindset at work to have mental peace and success at the work you do, and this will ultimately make you a productive person soon.

Productivity secret:

Never worry about results which undoubtedly occur at the end of any process. This will help you become stress-free at work.

30. Recharging Helps You Become Productive

"Recharging helps you accomplish more and stay active at work."
This is an easy productivity trick many people don't know, and this method is simple to use and have more influence at work and at making you productive. Recharging is a process which helps you gain more control over work by being able to stay focused on the work you do for a longer time.

Recharging isn't an unusually complicated thing you have to perform. It's basically a routine process which you can do, like any other task you perform in a day. The method of recharging is about doing something you love during breaks or when you feel bored with the work you are doing.

In the process of recharging your body and brain, you have to do few things to stay focused and interested in the work. The recharging of your physical body can be done by taking any food or drink which rejuvenates your body. You could come out of the workplace and inhale fresh air, and you could drink plenty of water, etc. to work continuously and effectively, you need to stay fit physically as well as mentally active and this could be only possible by taking necessary precautions.

There are several ways you could recharge your brain which is very necessary to work effectively. This recharging of your brain helps you stay focused on a particular task for a very longer time. Therefore it is very important to recharge your mind for productivity.

There are several ways you could charge your brain to stay focused and give productive results. They are as follows:

a. You could meditate or sit calm for at least 5-10 minutes during breaks.
b. Watch something really entertaining or inspiring during the breaks, and this will recharge your brain.
c. Take breaks when you get bored with the work you are doing, and this will help you have mental peace and prevent you from hating the work.
d. Listen to your favorite music or sing a song or play a musical instrument.

e. Drink a cup of tea or coffee.
f. Have a healthy diet every day, and this has a direct effect on your mind too and also on the physical body of yours.
g. Take small naps during breaks, and they have higher influence over your work. They actually charge you so much.
h. Stay exposed to the natural environment, and this will recharge your brain to work so effectively.

These are some of the very important ways which help you to recharge your brain which in turn helping your productive life. This recharging is a simple process which has wide capabilities when put into real use. You could explore the possibilities only by using the principle in real life and the more you use this recharging method, the stronger you will become physically as well as mentally.

Productivity secret:

> Try to take breaks when you get bored, and this recharges your mind and body.

31. Do Not Rush to Accomplish

"Never try to finish tasks in a hurry, which will give you bitter fruits from accomplishing any task."

The desire to complete the task so fast is good but the greed to complete task very quickly is atrocious. Many people are performers or doers, but the problem is this they always rush in accomplishing things so fast and end up with discouraging results all the time. Rushing to accomplish works will lead mostly to failures which are not what we wanted. Many people without thinking rush to accomplish a thing which is one of the reasons for failures. This way of doing things will result in losing confidence in the work we do and initially leads to the development of hate on work.

Accomplishing things is very important however never hurry at accomplishing things. Every task consumes a minimum amount of time, and you need to wait and stay still till a task completes and results are out. As we discussed in earlier chapters, never worry about results. Worrying about the results is the cause which makes you rush to accomplish things.

In rushing to accomplish things fast, we make many blunders which mostly fail us in finishing tasks correctly. There are several people in the modern world, who think that results should be obtained so fast and in the process, they lose patience and this patience is a very necessary component to have success in life.

The reason why most people hurry at accomplishing things is they may have various goals, and one more reason why they rush at accomplishing things is a lack of patience and as they believe mostly in shortcuts for success.

Hurry actually, hurts and can result in long-term consequences you have to face. You will end up missing moments of life if you continue to live like a zombie at work who just lives to finish tasks. You have got one precious life, and you will miss it, and at the end, you will regret your living way for sure.

Live your life slower and with patience and therefore the result is you become highly concentrated at work you do, and there are least or no errors possible when you work with a peaceful mindset.

To prevent this type of hurry at accomplishing things, practice to take the time to think before doing any work, and this will help you have a clear idea about work and aid you to work more efficiently.

As a result of working with the mental peace, you will do least mistakes and high output which can be considered to be productive. Always act thinking properly, and this will help you grow patience in you and also make you productive and successful.

One more way to refrain yourself from rushing at accomplishing things is by allotting a very decent amount of time to your tasks. This mostly try to use the allotted time, and this will help you work slower, and this gives your mind time to think, and this will surely help you change your way at work and makes you productive. You need to be very patient to see the change in you and find the desired outcome from the task you did.

Productivity secret:

Never perform any task in a hurry because the result will be mostly a failure.

32. Now and Later Charts Help you Become Better

"Now and Later charts helps you access your development and your future."

These charts are planning charts which help you visualize yourself at present as something great which you want to be in future. These charts help you to create strategic plans for future. These charts help you to find your present position and also help you assess your future position from your mind.

This way of now and late chart planning helps you make more effective ways to find success and have a more confident way of living in life. They act as a catalyst for an effective way of working to accomplish your goals or dreams.

There are many people, who made their lives better using this charts. In this charts, there is only factual information which helps you to build a strategy that separates the way you live today and later at someday of your life.

"You may seem to be nothing today, but you can be something tomorrow," this is what the now and later charts tell you. Realizing what they say makes you wise people who can make real changes in life that transform your way of living and bring you real success.

Always believe in change and transformation of lives which is very necessary for a better living and make real outcome from our beautiful life we are living. There are several things you should learn about yourself to have a clear idea of what you could do in your future and this will help you assess what you are? And when you find what you are it becomes easy to know what you have to be?

This way of finding you will help you build more effective strategic now and later charts which act as maps or guides for having a successful life. This way of planning helps you concentrate on vital things in your life, and this will help you work more efficiently and in turn, helps you become productive.

The reason why you need to build your own now, and later charts are as follows:

    a.   You will be able to visualize your success and make a difference of today and tomorrow.

b. Helps you build strong confidence levels, which is very necessary to work more efficiently.
c. You could create more effective plans, and it becomes easy to check progress as you know what and where you want to be in future. This helps you find how easily.
d. These charts also help you find your internal goals, dreams, and passion.
e. They help you concentrate more on work and make your work really lovable for you.
f. You could go from zero to something or something to everything. Now and later charts actually make you assess difference of living between you and others.
g. They also help you find out what you have accomplished and what you need to accomplish.

The above are some of the benefits you could get by making now and later charts. There are several possibilities using these charts at accomplishing your goals or dreams. They are easy to make, and they can be used to transform your conditions if they are making you fail every time in life.

These now and later charts are some special charts which help you find solutions and ways to excel in life. The charts are prepared as follows:

Step 1: draw a three column table in which the center column has more space.

Step 2: on the left column give heading as the present situation and on the right give heading as the future situation. The middle column is named as ways or ideas or solutions.

Step 3: construction of table is over, and now it's time to fill the table with appropriate words.

Step 4: on the left column which is named as present situation, write down your current situation. E.g.: I have started a company this year.

Step 5: on the right column which is named as future situation, write down what to want to accomplish or become. E.g.: I have to make my company the top 10 company till 2018

Step 6: in the middle column which is named as way/idea/solution/strategy, write down all possible ways to make you ultimate dream come alive. E.g.:

bring a number of clients by offers/create a productive working environment and bring more outcome etc.

Step 7: now you have completed filling the now and later chart and have a look at the chart every day and find a new innovative solution to make your dream come alive.

This is the simple way you could make use of building efficient now and later charts which guide you to take right actions and become more productive.

1. Example of now and later chart for accomplishing a dream or goal:

Present situation	Strategy/way/idea/solution	Future situation
I started a company this year	bring a number of clients by offers/create an effective working environment and bring more outcome or do more marketing etc.	Make my company reach top 10 place
Present situation	Strategy/way/idea/solution	Future situation
I lost my job	Ask my friends about the availability of job/ research all places where I could find a job I love to do.	I want this particular job

2. Example for Now and Later chart for solving a problem

Present situation	Strategy/way/idea/solution	Future situation
I am a normal man/ women	Learn to sing and practicing more and learning from mistakes	I am a singer

3. Example for finding ways to execute your dream/goal

The above are the examples for now and later charts, and you could use them in practical use. These charts are also used for several other purposes, and they have a broad range of capabilities which help you think more to solve a problem or accomplish a big thing in life.

Try using these charts in your practical life and find solutions easily. They are several people who used these charts to make their lives better, and you could use them too. Have belief in you to make anything a possibility.

One of my students shared his experience of how he got improved results in his life using this now and later chart. He is an average student who has the problem of concentration in his studies, and this made him get fewer grades and one day after a session he approached me and explained his problem and asked for a solution.

I gave him a template of this now a later chart which has all headings printed. Now I told him to write down his problem in column 1 that is in the present situation and write what he wants to be by solving his problem in colum3 that is the future situation. I told him to come with ideas or ways to make his future situation possible.

I also gave him a trick that is thinking about all the barriers that made him fail to concentrate and then write solutions that help you face those hurdles, and he did as I said. Then I told him that's over. He said what? I told him it's that simple you have found your own solutions. Try those solutions you made and give me your feedback to my mail. I handed my card and left, and after 2 weeks I received a letter expressing his success.

Productivity secret:

> Comparing now and then helps you find progress and
> helps you become more productive.

Now and later charts help you frame a plan to become something in future.

33. Work Alone is not Important

*"Life is not just about keeping working.
It has several things you should actually pursue."*

This is very important to realize in life. This rule is mainly meant for work alcoholics. There are several people, who just keep working all the way ignoring living, moments, celebrations, family, etc. there are several people who just keep working not showing interest in their living and believe me no one lives forever. Everyone has to die someday and therefore living the life which has everything is very important.

You may not have one more chance to live this human life. Now you have one and just concentrate on things that make you happier and also your work to. But too much working is not at all good, and you will regret your life at the end if you just concentrate only on your work.

I have seen people who consistently work to have more money in their life and even though they had got enough money they never stop constantly working as it became their habit and this led them to lose their valuable life for nothing. These people don't care their relations, celebrations, family, friends, etc. they only care about their work. These people may be successful, but whoever they may be they will surely hate their living ways at the end. You should not become the one.

One more important thing is always working doesn't make you productive. You need to show your interest in certain things that help you gain mental peace, happiness, and satisfaction which will help you gain more mental energy to work faster. This way of living also could make you successful and productive.

Productivity is just about bringing more outcomes in short period using fewer efforts. This is only possible by living every moment of life. The moments in life are only possible by living your life spending more with others at least start spending time with your family, and this will help you build strong relationships and also helps you gain more mental control and peace. This is what called as real satisfied living.

Whatever work it may be you are doing? And how much work it may be you are doing? Nothing is so important than your mental peace. Do you work and you may need to spend a lot of time n your work but remember to spend at least few minutes of time with your family and in celebrations. This will not only give you happiness but also mental peace which is a necessary asset to concentrate more on you work and get work finished in time. Even this way of working can be considered as productive.

This story of a man has inspired me to grow stronger belief in this principle. In the story, this man is really a guy whose behavior reflects many our behavior at work. According to the story, the man is purely a workaholic who only shows priority to work he did and neglected his family and life. He is successful, but he has no peace and happiness in his life. He had got a family which has three members, the wife and two children and these three love him so much. Even he loves them but never showed it to them as he always showed priority to work he does. He never realized the importance of giving more priority to his family is very important than family. However, he never spent time with his family any day thinking that he never had time. He never showed interest in celebrations as is busy always with work. He never traveled so much as he is reserved with the work but a day has come in his life which changed his life completely and made him a different person than before what he is.

One day he was going to his office in the car, and suddenly a van dashed him so hard that he is severely injured and got admitted to the hospital. He felt like it was his last day. Suddenly every moment of his life he had got in front of his eyes running in his brain. He regretted his way of living in which only work is being given priority.

He received treatment at the hospital and took about two weeks to recover from injuries, and the whole two weeks his family is with him take all care necessary. After two weeks of time, he is able to get up from the bed and able to walk now. So he is discharged from the hospital and came back to his home.

It took few more weeks to recover completely from injuries and become normal. The family took great care of him till he got recovered. This is the only time he has spent all his time with the family. This time is really important time for him which taught him a very important thing in his life. He realized the importance of life. He is able to realize the importance of family in life.

That accident changed his lifestyle and taught him a very important lesson for his life.

After getting recovered, he decided to spend his little time with the family along with the work but the important thing is he realized to which priority has to be given in life than work that is family. This one simple change of priority changed his lifestyle completely. It is really surprising to his family that he is spending time with the family and taking his breakfast and dinner with his family every day after getting recovered from the accident. He calls home and talks when he is at work. All these new traits of behavior surprised the family but all they are happy with such wonderful way of their living their lives together.

Many people ignore family, relations and happy moments in life by giving priority to their work which is always a false way of becoming productive. The most important rule to becoming productive is to have a peaceful mindset which is only possible to people who actually live their lives.

Work will bring only results that bring you money, fame, and sometimes happiness but your family, relations, celebrations and achievements bring you happiness and satisfaction in life. Realize this rule and work efficiently and this will help you become productive.

These are few tips for to use to become really productive at living your life which is full of wonderful memories.

a. Spend time traveling to different places. There are several excellent places you should visit in your lifetime and write down the places you should visit and start exploring the outer world around you.

b. Spend time on celebrating your success, and this boosts your mental energy to accomplish more great things.

c. Spend time with selected people who can really understand you and this will help you bring out all your internal feelings and dreams to share. You could share your happiness and sadness which helps your brain to become balanced.

d. Go camping in a forest with your friends and enjoy the nature. It always inspires you to live naturally and more efficiently.

e. Create priorities for things that make you happy, and this will help you gain more control over life.

- f. Try meeting your relations and make a very good time spending together happily.
- g. Try visiting a peaceful place, and this will help you gain mental peace which will make you happy.
- h. Spend your time with family, and this will help you build strong relations and create a happy living.

All the above tips help you live a real life which is full of happiness and satisfaction. These tips also help you grow more power to excel at the work by helping you create mental peace. Always make time for important things in life other than work which is very important in human life. This life is short and wonderful which cannot be explained by anyway. Try to make your life meaningful living it as a legend and create memories that last longer and helps you love your life at the end.

There are several people, who are attention is drawn to work immediately, and this is how they are unable to spend their time on other important things in life which made them stick to work longer and become workaholics. For this type of people, there are several ways you could get distracted from the work and spend living your life on some other things. These are the following tips you could make use of to maintain your time for other important things in life.

- a. Get disconnected from the work. This can be done by getting away from the work environment or place.
- b. Get disconnected from the technology. This is what draws most people attention and make them fail to pursue their lives. Therefore stay away from your technology devices. Don't attend any calls and emails. Stay calm and keep spending time on other things.
- c. Complete works in steps, and this will help you allot time for other things in life.
- d. Create proper timetables and to do lists in which some amount of time is allotted for other things in life.
- e. Take breaks in work and stay calm at that time and this will recharge your body and brain and help you finish tasks faster, and this will save time for other things in life.
- f. Maintain self-control by taking all necessary precautions, and this will help you have control over external things.

Productivity secret:

Only work don't fulfill your living, and there are several things you need to experience in your life to be called as a productive person.

Spend time for something which will help you grow interest, in life.

34. CREATIVE WORKS VERSUS FORMAL WORKS

"Creative works and formal works are two types of works which you should pursue."

These are two types of work which influence our productivity levels. These are two different types of tasks which determine our success of life. Creative works require more thinking, and formal works need more efforts. The difference between them helps you to assess the success. The major differences between these two types of works are as follows mentioned below.

Creative works are formal or informal works that help you do things in a unique way. These creative works play a major role in success as they are what influence the world. Formal works are the routine tasks that are always boring if performed for longer periods. These formal works may not be unique.

Creative works require more thinking skills and requires an uncertain amount of time but success is for sure which is unlimited whereas formal works require more or less time which requires the knowledge of doing a process and success is very limited from formal or routine tasks.

Creative works are the works you will find interesting in doing whereas formal or routine tasks are boring and usual tasks which make you lose interest. The reason why you should know the differences between creative works and formal works is to help you realize their power which helps you become productive.

These are the two types of works which we generally have to accomplish in our daily lives, and this chapter helps you to create priority over these tasks, and this will help you which are important to do to get real success. This assessment helps you become productive easily.

This is how you should give priority to two different types of works. Creative works bring you more success than routine works. Give first priority to them, and they may consume less or more, but success is for sure. It's like accomplish one great thing than several small things.

To become really productive and successful, do creative works first and then do routine works later. An additional tip would be hiring someone to perform routine tasks and o creative works by yourself if you can hire and pay. This helps you save more time for your creative works, and your mind will stay active longer.

Creative tasks inspire us to concentrate and work more. This way of working always produces effective results. Therefore consider accomplishing creative works first and routine works later. This will add up to live a productive life

Many great personalities and influences in the world know this secret, and they have made success by giving priority to accomplish creative tasks. These creative tasks may be our dreams, goals or passion. You will always find happiness, satisfaction and mental peace in accomplishing them.

Always give priority to creative tasks fast then routine tasks to become productive.

Productivity secret:

Creative works need more mental energy and less physical energy. Formal or casual works need high physical energy and less mental energy.

35. Convert Morning Time to Productive Time

"Morning time has fewer disturbances which help you concentrate more and longer."

Early Morning time can be called as Magical time. This magical time has several advantages. This is generally early in the morning the magical time begins. This time is a very precious time which you need to make use of very carefully. Human life is shot and wonderful which is influenced by time factor so much and therefore time has given a greater value regarding measuring success and greatness gained through accomplishments utilizing the time properly.

When it comes to time in the early morning, it's more precious time than any other time period in a day. This time when used correctly makes you highly productive and successful. This time for doing your work helps you save more daytime which can be used to accomplish many more goals and dreams.

Do you know that? This early morning time helps you to work faster and effectively. The one more secret you have to know is this time helps you stay very active physically and mentally all the day. This is the time where you can breathe less polluted oxygen necessary for your brain to stay healthy and active.

Use this morning time to build your physical body and do exercises for physical and mental improvement of your body. This will help you have a healthy life. This time can make you stay fit. This is the reason why many sportsmen and women, yoga teachers, etc. use the time for teaching, learning and practicing things that construct a better life for future.

Even businessmen, authors, artists, doctors, etc. whoever they may be regarding profession who are successful, happy and satisfied with their lives are people whose day starts early in the morning.

Now I hope you have realized the very importance of early morning time. Try to make use of this valuable time for important works, and this will help you become productive. It's your turn to make your success possible through taking the initiative in utilizing the time very properly.

In chapter 1, there is a little explanation about the importance of early morning, and you can have a glance at it if you wish to learn the importance. The morning time has a greater importance to accomplish great thing quickly.

To become productive, use this time to accomplish very important things. This time is suitable mainly for creative tasks as you can focus more during this period on your work. You can also do more work during this stage.

This morning time has fewer disturbances and therefore helps you concentrate easily. Therefore this time must be allotted to very important tasks. This is the time where your thoughts are more in control as it is the time that starts after you wake up. This time can be considered as the time which comes after our body gets charged both physically and mentally during sleep. The morning time is a very productive time which you have to realize.

This is the time you are highly energized, motivated and inspired and relaxed and therefore this is the very precious time you could make use of to produce great outcome through fewer efforts.

To make more out of this productive morning time, plan ahead in advance that is during the night before the new day arrives. This will help you go to sleep with full hopes and helps you get inspired to live another day according to plan and bring out outcome and success which can be considered as productivity.

To make more out of this early morning time, you can start the day by doing the work you love, and this will help you stay inspired longer in a day which is very important to make real memories for life.

To find out whether this early morning time is productive. We did a little experiment in which we asked a group of people to live in two different conditions. The first condition is they have to wake up early in the morning and start doing their work and then their feedback of how productive they are should be reported.

In the second condition, they can sleep longer as they wish and should get up early in the morning and start working and feedback should be given about how much productive they are along with how they felt all day.

In the first condition, the group of reported high productivity levels and they are a very active whole day which is what we thought and the in the second condition the productivity is not what we thought. It's really random. The productivity level feedback we got is very random, and it is different to different people. Many people in this condition showed positive results, but the one thing it lacked is these people are not active as they were in the first condition.

Even feedback is really different in both the conditions. The people in group conditions gave good feedback, and in second group it's uncertain. Therefore to find real benefits of this early morning time working, we have interviewed this group of people about how they felt in two different conditions. The feedback is taken regarding satisfaction levels which helped us as a proof for high productivity levels that happened in the first condition that is in the Magical morning time.

In the first condition the satisfaction levels are really awesome, and in the second condition, the satisfaction levels are lower on an average which helped us understand the power of magical morning time.

Your outcome may be good in both the conditions, but you cannot be considered productive unless you gain the mental satisfaction of work you do because productivity is a long term process and a magical habit only few can acquire. Therefore to become productive always use this magical morning time for accomplishing important tasks.

Productivity secret:

> Morning time has fewer disturbances and is the perfect time for performing very important things in life.

PART THREE

36. Take This Weapon Wherever you go

"Discipline helps you gain self-control that helps you gain control over life."

I call this a weapon of staying productive for a long time. Remember to take this along with you all the time to stay productive all the time. This is one secret weapon which will help you grow self-respect and self-control. This is a very simple weapon you already know. It is Discipline.

This chain shows the way to get a thin weapon. The chain is as follows:

Self-respect + Self-control → Discipline

The following chain helps you understand how you can grow self-discipline in you which will make you productive. One who has self-discipline can have more control over external factors in which time is one factor. If you have control over it, you can be considered as productive. This one simple way could help you grow faster and have mental peace and satisfaction at work you do.

Discipline is something spectacular habit that makes human understand things in a systematic manner, and this way of understanding approach helps in building strong control over subject and work. This helps us build stronger mindset which is very useful for strong will power which helps you stay longer with problems and work which helps you gain success easily.

Knowing the importance of having discipline helps you to grow in you and this discipline, in turn, helps your build stronger mindset for accomplishing things and this will make you productive. This discipline helps you maintain your mind stay symmetric in thinking which produces best decisions in the world. Always carry this weapon in your life to gain good habits and stick to those good habits longer.

A disciple is defined as the process of training your mind to obey rules and code which help you always stay in control without going wrong in any way. The important thing you have to understand is about control. Control is not just a term with some meaning in practical life. It is, in fact, a more important thing which has influence over work life financial life, personal life, and productivity life.

This control over things is only possible to a great extent by developing discipline in you. Therefore disciple has very importance to have control over your work and control over several other aspects of life. So there is a high necessity to develop discipline in you to manage your work and life.

The system of discipline acts this way in gaining control over things. Developing discipline helps you stay in control, and this self-control ability helps you to gain over the external environment, and the helps you achieve success. It's that simple system which can make you realize the importance of discipline in productivity life. It can be shown in the form of the simple chain as follows. Develop Discipline – helps in gaining self-control- self-control helps you gain control over external environment – control over environment gives you success.

Many people lack discipline which is the reason why they fail many times in their lives. These people lack control over things in their life, and this is the reason why they are considered to be unproductive. If you really want to excel at your work and life, develop discipline in your life which makes you productive.

Productivity secret:
>Discipline helps you stay in control and this, in turn,
>helps you have control over the external world.

37. SMALL LISTS WORK BETTER

"When you feel something difficult, big and complex, try small."

Small lists are handy lists you could use to feel your day and work very simple. These are general handy lists which contain most important works to accomplish. The tasks are generally given a high priority in your life to get succeeded. The most amazing thing about these small lists is they are really handy and helps you concentrate more on important tasks and therefore helps to accomplish the tasks and become productive.

The reason why you need to know the importance of these small lists is they are really useful for achieving short term goals with the high outcome. These lists can be a piece of paper or a card which is really handy for you. They are easy to fit in your palm, and this cards or lists contain a very few number of goals which helps you to concentrate on important things first. This way of giving priority to tasks help you accomplish your important goals first which makes you real productive.

Generally, these lists are used for accomplishing goals however they can be used effectively to do your daily tasks in time which is crucial to become productive. Preparing these lists is very easy and quick. It's actually fun creating these lists, and you get highly satisfied when you accomplish tasks in the list.

The lists are generally prepared by giving priority to your important tasks. The lists help you concentrate more on things which make you productive and enjoyable. They have greater influence over your productive life. It's very easy to make small lists for your daily routine life and make most out of it. The process of creating short lists can be explained as follows in steps.

Step 1: Cut the paper into a small piece which can fit into your palm. Even you can use a card for making these short lists. The card is preferred to paper as it lasts longer than paper.

Step 2: now it's time to bring out your creative side of mind to make your card look beautiful. Design the card in a beautiful way which makes you feel inspired. If you are not good at art, you could find designs online and take print of them. The reason why these cards should look beautiful is that our mind has the habit of getting attracted to beauty and gets inspired. This way of making cards helps you have pleasant mood when you look at the card, and this will help you concentrate more on tasks in the card which force our mind to work on tasks or goals. Your beautiful templates are ready to be in use for our list making.

Step 3: write down all the tasks you have to do in a day in a separate paper. This is done as we have to make several revised lists and use a normal paper for filtering the task list. This will help you filter your to-do list or to accomplish list shorter and effective which will help you concentrate more on what is important.

Step 4: after finishing filtering the list, take only top 5 important tasks you have to accomplish and enter them into the designed template card and place it in your pocket and have a watch at it when you want to get inspired to accomplish the tasks in the list. This will help you have an active mind for accomplishing your goals and have success in life. These cards may look simple, but they have much influence in practical use which is what you have to realize.

Productivity secret:

> When size matters, think small. Always make use of small lists to plan better and accomplish better.

38. Rapport Methods for Transformation

"Copy the best methods to gain best success."

Rapport methods can be useful to transform your way of living whether it may be productive or unproductive. If it is productive, it gets optimized, and if it isn't productive, it becomes productive. This is the very specialty of this method.

Rapport methods are nature oriented methods which have a natural effect on people to become productive. The natural effect is based on how you react by copying the nature or living organisms. This method relies on human nature to get things done by mirroring others. It's common nature that human copies best things or methods and apply them in real life situations to get success.

This kind of human's natural behavior can be applied to learning best methods or effective ways to get productive and success. This chapter is purely based on human nature of copying things for getting success easily. To get most of this chapter you need to understand the natural behavior of human at copying things in his life. This way of understanding gives you clear idea of using this chapter in your practical life.

We actually love rapport with nature. We love fantasy and fantasy is based on our real life situations and the environment. We many wish to fly like birds, we wish to stay strong like a lion or we wish to become invisible like air, etc. we always try to rapport with nature even in our imagination irrespective of whether it is truth or not. Many people follow a single system by copying each other, and the copying process happens by analyzing the source we copy. If the source is good, we copy, and if it is bad, we reject. This is how our internal copying system works.

The system of a particular type of ways is being built by influences, and people follow it blindly because they believe that influencers are always right. Influencers are successful people whose ideas proved what they are? Therefore the proofs of their success make them influencers and the remaining world, the followers. It's like following the leader to have a better life.

Let's take the example of powerful leaders in the world. They are exceptional at influencing the people, and this is possible by the way they make their living unique. Therefore this rapport method helps you get success in an easy way by following the methods of living of successful people or influencers or leaders.

This rapport system runs in a simple way which helps you establish long-term success. This rapport system also helps you to become productive. Follow the system and this chain helps to understand the process of people using the rapport to gain success in their life too.

Follower/Copier – attracted to success - methods that gave success - role model/leader/influencer/source of copy.

In the chain, the rapport happens because of our desire to gain success. We get attracted to success first then to the person who gained success and then we start exploring the ways that gave success and this is how the success of rapport happens in practical life.

Rapport the model/source/person who you think is productive and successful and this way of rapport are possible by copying the ways or methods of them which helped them gain success. Copy and paste all the ways that led to success and productive life, and this will help you transform your life easily in less time.

Just watch the people who are productive and successful. Then research about their lifestyle and principles which built their attitude towards work and life. This will help you assess their behavior and also learn all the methods used by them to gain success This will help you learn complex things in a simple way and these can be applied in your practical life to become productive and get success.

Many people have role models in their life. However, not everyone follows the model. It is surprising that many people take someone as a role model but they never follow them, and that is why they can't reach their goals. It's not a rule to follow the role model but to understand how they function to accomplish things in their life is very important. This understanding gives you access to new ideas and thoughts to excel in a subject you are interested in your life. This is how you learn and apply success principles in your life easily.

This same method applies to gain productivity life. The reason why you need to copy productivity principles of your role model is that they have gained success after great trials and pain and by copying your role model you may get ready to face every obstacle in your path easily and find success. It is very necessary to realize that all successful people may not be productive keep this in mind that is all productive people are successful. This is the reason why you need to rapport your role model to gain success easily.

This is the process you can rapport your role model and learn from him or her, and it can be explained in steps as follows:

Step 1: select your one role model

Select a role model and learn about him/her life clearly. Find every step he or she took to reach that level, and this will help you have a clear idea of how success became possible for him/her.

Step 2: research for ideas and ways

In this step find all the ways and ideas used by your role model and this way of finding can be done by re-engineering. This gives you ideas and thoughts of how you could make your success possible.

Step 3: now write down all methods, ways, ideas, and thoughts and put them to use and this will help you have clear successful methods for your success and become productive.

This 3 step process is simple and effective. Use it practically, and you will find perfect ways for your success soon, and you can put into use so fast and become productive.

Productivity secret:

> Learn from others and learn best methods for work to easily become productive and successful.

39. CCMU Method Works Great

"Copy and morph the best methods in a way that is applicable to your needs."

This method is very simple to use if you get excel at using the rapport method because this can be considered as an extension of rapport method. In rapport method, we copy ideas, ways, methods and thoughts and put them into use directly and therefore few methods may be not great for your use due to lack of proper situations and therefore there has to be improved methods from existing methods, or there is a requirement of whole new methods. This method is mainly for improving existing methods or give rise to whole new methods which can be used in a very effective manner, and this method helps you develop new improved methods easily.

Go back to the last chapter and read it clearly to understand this chapter clearly, as these two chapters are interlinked.

CCMU stands for cut, copy, morph and use. This method can be explained by explaining the four terms. These terms give you clear idea of how this method works and you can consider these terms as steps for this method. The terms can be explained as follows:

Step 1: Cut

The term cut in this method refers to mining out methods and ways of success from your role model. This step can only be performed after proper research about your role model's success

Step 2: Copy

This term is about writing down or recording the mined out successful principles or methods or ways, and this is just a copying process. This process is explained in the last chapter clearly.

Step 3: Morph

Now all the methods or ways for success are with you, and they may work more efficiently if certain changes are made to the methods and the changes made are an improvement we make to upgrade the methods. These methods can only be made if you really understand the methods and ways very clearly.

Step 4: Use

This step or term is about putting your methods into action to bring out the outcome. In the method the improved methods or newly created methods are put into practical use and trials are made to find how successful they are.

This CCMU method is very simple to understand but requires little efforts to make more out of it. This method helps you become productive by establishing a connection you with your passion or work or goal and your role model's ideas, methods, and ways. This is how you can become successful utilizing this method.

Productivity secret:

> It's better to create your own method, and the easiest way would transform a perfect method to work for you.

40. How to Stop Over Thinking?

"Over thinking is one of the biggest barriers to productive life."

Over thinking is the biggest barrier to your productive life and success. This is a very important barrier you should take care of before it's too late. Over thinking is a bad habit and one of the top reason people becoming procrastinators. The effects of over thinking are: over thinking kills productivity, it kills your dreams and goals, it kills happiness and peace, it makes you procrastinate, etc.

There are several problems caused due to over thinking, and therefore it is considered as a productivity barrier you have to face in your life to become productive and successful. This helps you live a stress-free life in addition to becoming productive.

One of my acquaintances had this habit of over thinking, and she had faced a great loss in her life because of this habit, and she became a procrastinator in time and hated the way she lived her life. After some time she decided to change the way she was living her life and then she started trying different solutions to get rid of her boring life and live a new wonderful life.

After researching a lot, she found that over thinking was what made her a procrastinator which she found out by reverse engineering process. She wrote all reasons why she quit her works or goals or passion projects and over thinking is the top reason she came up with. She came up with a plan which she named life transformation plan.

In the transformation plan, she wrote all the solutions to prevent procrastinating habit and over thinking. This plan is considered to be effective when used properly, and the improvement is measured every week. Whenever she feels that her thinking is out of control, she takes a break from it. She gets disconnected with the thinking process. This is the plan she had used.

Thinking is a process which produces thoughts. When this thinking leads to the production of negative thoughts, it's the sign of brain undergoing over thinking process. This is the point you have to distract your brain and make it concentrate on the positive thoughts, and this will help you stay focused on your goal or dream, and it becomes possible to accomplish your goal or dream.

Your thinking can be changed at the point of over thinking by concentrating on what inspire you so much every day in life, and this will help you get over your over thinking habit and helps you get success and become productive. This way of change in life makes you a doer rather than a procrastinator.

This is how you can transform your life by preventing over thinking habit in your path of success, and this will help you transform your life into a successful, productive and satisfied life. There are several other solutions you could find out for yourself to prevent over-thinking and become productive. Over thinking is a mental barrier which causes several severe problems in getting success and therefore learned to hack your over thinking habit to make a real success in life.

Productivity secret:

Over-thinking is one of the biggest mental barriers which make people become procrastinators.

Think till your brain produce positive thoughts and when it starts producing negative thoughts. Stop thinking and start working

41. How to Prevent Fear And Kill Doubts?

"Fear kills productive life and success. Doubts fuel your fear"

Fear makes you stay idle without performing your duties. This fear has several dangerous effects on the success of people. Fear kills creativity, your productive life and can make you live a horrible life. It is so surprising that several great works are accomplished with a little fear in an individual. Fear is always residing in an individual but allow speaking it for yourself which mostly fails you to excel.

Fear can create limitless flaws in an individual's behavior and finally makes you stressful which ultimately leads to unproductive life. Fear is the top reason why most people fail in accomplishing things. Fear can make you lose confidence and can make you feel your survival tough. This can destroy one's peace. There are unlimited ways fear destroys us in many ways. Therefore it is very important to understand to effects of failure and learn how to tackle fear in real life. This will help you live more easily with the stress-free mind.

If you really want to live your life, you must leave fear in life because fear causes death every second of your life and it's your turn to decide whether to die every second of your life or live an incredible fearless life.

There are several types of fear which causes you unproductive. Fear of failure, fear of taking risks, fear of survival, fear caused due to an inferiority complex, fear of imagining success. These are top 5 fears which make people unproductive and also make them procrastinate and fail at getting success.

Curing these fears in you automatically makes you force your mind to concentrate on accomplishing your goals. This will help you become productive life and fear is a mental illusion which has to be cured as soon as possible.

As fear is an illusion, the derivatives of it are also illusions which you have to face with to become productive. The top 5 fears that make you unproductive are mentioned above and can be explained as follows:

a. Fear of failure
    This is the top type which makes most of the people in world unproductive and lives unsatisfied lives. This fear of failure is caused by you because

of consistent failures in your life, or they are induced in you by people around you through their advice or suggestions. This makes you not to take any further steps to try things in life. Fear of failure stops you to accomplish tasks by acting as a barrier which is very difficult to overcome for anyone. This makes you become a procrastinator.

This illusion can be broken by realizing the truth t there is nothing to lose and the loss only happens if you don't take actions and the only way to kill fear of failure in you is by becoming a doer. Start accomplishing tasks right away without thinking too much and this will help you flow only positive thoughts in your brain which helps you become a doer from a procrastinator. This is one natural method you can use of to kill fear of failure in you. There are several people, who have this fear of failure, and therefore this should be prevented to become productive.

b. Fear of taking risks

This is the second type of fear which makes you unproductive. This fear may not make you live a horrible life, but I promise you that you are going to live an unsatisfied, boring and compromised life forever. This fear makes you not to take any risks which could attain you a great position and make success possible in your life. This type of fear is mainly gained due to limiting ourselves and by suggestions of others. If you don't take risks, you won't get something fruitful, and this is the fact.

To face this fear stop comparing yourself with others and stop limiting yourself and one more thing you have to do never listen to others advice and get compromised with your goals and dreams. This is the only way you could face this fear and gain success as well as fear.

c. Fear of survival

This is very natural fear most of the people have in this world. This is programmed fear by nature. Nature teaches us to survive by anyway. And this is the reason we always have a fear of survival. Our mind always thinks to survive at a place by some way and suddenly it becomes against to your consciousness, and this is how fear of survival expands its influence in the human brain.

As survival is at the main pace, our mind stops trying new things to make our survival constant and balanced but believe me there is no such thing as balanced survival. Nature always changes and situations always change in life and the methods of survival changes too. If you keep compromising your life, you cannot live a wonderful life. This fear makes you productive but in a limited manner and this is not fair. Break the rule or limit in your mind and always try to attain great place than thinking about your survival and not taking any actions.

No one knows what happens next moment and just thinking about what happens next and sitting just like that doesn't improve your life. Keep doing things and forget about survival as it can be gained for sure by taking confident actions into work for you. This will help you become productive and live a satisfied and uncompromised life.

d. Fear caused due to inferiority complex

Inferiority complex is a routinely listened term which is really important to discuss to become productive and successful. As this fear is caused due to an inferiority complex, it can only be cured by curing inferiority complex.

Inferiority complex is a situation where you feel low. You lack confidence which is necessary to start and finish any work. This inferiority complex makes you think negative all the time and makes you a pessimist. This soon turns you into a procrastinator. You will never make any trials to accomplish things. You will have boring and unsatisfied lives. There are several effects caused by fear which is caused due to an inferiority complex.

When this feeling of inferiority takes away one's life, this results in inferiority complex. This is mainly formed by comparing yourself with others. Comparing yourself to others is a big mistake you could make, and this will make you start to feel lower and ultimately this result in loss of self-confidence and self-respect which are necessary components for accomplishing any work. When you lack these components, you ultimately become unproductive.

Therefore stop comparing yourself with others and always stay confident and inspired. This way of change in you helps you to kill inferiority complex formed in you and therefore you will have a wonderful life which always gives you right fruits at the right time.

Realize that you are unique. If you think you are not unique, at least something in you is different from others which make you unique and therefore comparing will not make your life better and judging your life by comparison always produce wrong judgments which get you live a horrible life which is full of pain and failures.

There are several people in this world, who have this inferiority complex and learn to control it before it starts controlling you and this will help you kill the fear caused due to an inferiority complex in you and become productive.

e. Fear of imagining success

This is the surprising type of fear which most people have in their minds. We have already read about fear of failure, but this is the time you need to understand about fear of imagining success.

This fear is caused by imagining the final result or outcome produced by accomplishing a task. Thinking about the future outcome and concentrating more on it than the process you are pursuing will give you this fear. This fear is developed due to a comparison between outcome imagined and measured process which is going on. The only way to prevent this fear is to stop thinking about results or success which always happens at the end. This type of thinking will make your mind stressful if your work you are doing doesn't meet your expectation results and as a result, you become unproductive. Therefore stop imagining about results and just concentrate on the work you do and this will help you become productive.

The fear can produce doubts which become barriers to moving forward in any work. When you cure these 5 types of fear you could easily minimize or kill these doubts and become productive for sure.

Productivity secret:

Fear is one biggest barrier which destroys your productive life.

To prevent fear, you need to stop worrying about it and start working.

42. Minimizing Addictions

"Addictions can help you pass the time in vain and also effects you by not allowing finishing your tasks on time."

Addictions are also the barriers which make you unproductive and lazy at work you do or at accomplishing things. These are the constraints which make you live like a programmed robot or zombie lives for one thing they are addicted too. These addictions make no difference between human and a programmed robot. Addictions can cause several errors in a productive life and cause you fail at accomplishing your goals or dreams.

These addictions are formed as a result of sticking our life to less important things which can be called as bad habits give rise to these addictions. When the same process happens with good habits, they become principles of success. These two can be understood by the chains below. The chains give your clear idea of the difference between principles of success and principle of failure (Addictions).

Stick to the good habits longer → principles of life → gives success

Stick to the bad habits longer → principles of failure (Addictions) → gives failure

Therefore addictions can be called as the principles of failure. However, these addictions are not easy to overcome as they are formed as a result of the long-term process of sticking with them for a longer time. Minimizing these addictions is very necessary to become productive.

Addictions can make you lose time as they consume most of your productive time which is why you fail at accomplishing tasks. Addictions make you lose your valuable life to do unimportant tasks all your life, and at the end of life, it makes you regret your own life for being addicted to things in life.

Therefore addictions have to be cured to not only become productive and successful but also to live a life you always love. Addictions are the complex type of interruptions which stay longer in life. Addictions are easy to cure but take a lot of time and efforts. There are several addictions in this modern world which are consuming up the productive time of people.

In the modern world different individuals are addicted to different things. Few are addicted to the internet. Few are addicted to watching TV. Few others are addicted to social media. Few others are addicted to technology gadgets such as mobiles, PC, etc. whatever type the addiction may be the result is just you become unproductive and lazy. These addictions are easy to overcome only when you create a stronger belief to change or transform your life.

These addictions can only be cured in you by changing your mind directions to positive things which actually produce some outcome, and this will help you become productive as well as free from addictions. Just start doing something rather than sitting doing nothing or sticking to some bad habit. This will help you get diverted from the addictions and work on something very important.

Productivity secret:

Addictions make you fail at concentrating at work.

Addictions can be prevented or cured by taking small steps to change you.

43. Follow this Golden Principle

"There are two ways you could do the work by heart. One is doing the work you love and another is love the work you do."

This only golden principle could actually make you live a wonderful life which is productive as well as successful. This principle makes you a real human who can transform things in life. This also helps you to work to fullest to give perfect results.

The principle is very simple and cute one you will love all your life if you make use of it in your practical life. The principle is as quoted below:

"Do the work you love and love the work you do."

The reason why people fail at accomplishing a task is that they actually don't love the work they do and this results in the unproductive behavior of performer. Therefore it is very important to do the work you love, and this is what makes your life satisfying as you are living to accomplish your dreams or goals in life.

There are many people, who complain that there is nothing they actually love doing, and some people complain that they love the work they do, but sometimes they hate doing the work they love. If you are any of these criteria, then you could use these solutions to excel at the work you do.

If you have no work that you love, then it's time to start loving the work you do because you have work to survive and survival is very important than searching for the work you love and therefore start enjoying your work, and this will help you work more efficiently. The only way to love your work is by understanding its importance and your role in accomplishing it. Learn more tricks to work more efficiently and learn all possible skills which will help you excel at your work, and this will help you find your love for work you do that is you can grow love over work you do.

If you are doing the work you love but not satisfied at all, then it's time to search for satisfaction in your work. Find all the reasons why you are unsatisfied with your work, and this will help you grow clear love over the work you do. If you fail to find satisfaction, then you will soon end up hating the work you do.

There is something for everyone who makes you lack satisfaction and always find and solve it before it produces negative effects on you.

I always suggest you do the work you love and if due to improper situations you fail at doing what you love then just stick to what you can do at that moment and this will help you survive and get prepared to perform what you love when proper situation arises.

There are several people who compromised with their work at first and waited for the moment of inspiration which helped them pursue their passion or goal or dream. So never keep waiting doing nothing. Do something all the time, and when opportunity knocks the door just grabs it, and this will make you love the work you do and live a wonderful life. This is how you could become productive at work using the wonderful principle stated above.

Productivity secret:

Do the work you love to become productive and successful.

Love the work you do to find passion in your work and love it.

44. WORKING REPEATEDLY IS NOT RIGHT

"Working continuously makes your work seem so boring and therefore take breaks frequently."

There are many people, who work continuously, and as a result, they gain a lot of money, and you can call the unsatisfied money hunters. They are the one who works for money leaving about finding their life purpose. These people don't realize that work alone is not important in life. This is why they keep working, and these are considered to be workaholics. These may gain success but its unsatisfied success. They may increase happiness but its unsatisfied happiness. They always get incomplete satisfaction from their accomplishments.

The reason why their success remains incomplete is that due to continuously working they lose their valuable things in life such as their relations, family, celebrations, etc. in the process, they even lose time which is actually should be used to accomplish their goals or dreams.

This one human life is incredible and wonderful thing which should be lived to the full extent. We may not get one more life like this and therefore don't waste it on unimportant things or just on only one important thing. It should be a collection of different memories and experiences. Never make it worthless by doing trivial things all the way of your life.

There are several things you could do with your life. Don't stick to just one thing. You could use it to accomplish your goals and dreams, or you could use it for a good cause. You could use it to create something that helps the world become a better place for living. There are numerous possibilities you could do with your life. Therefore don't use it just for working all the way.

There is a lot to discover in your life by living it in the way you wished to be. You could do several things in your life. Live every way you could, and this will help you live a wonderful life which is full of energy, hope, and enthusiasm. To get disconnected from work you can do the following things.

You could go on a tour, or you could go on vacation with your family, or you could listen to songs or you could watch a movie you love and the important thing is to relax as much as possible. Working continuously may not give high output most of the times and if you start taking breaks between your work it helps you recharge your body and mind and therefore you can work longer and better.

This way of working continuously makes you hate the work some day along with the disaster that happens as mentioned above. Therefore take frequent breaks while working, you could take naps to get relaxed. You could spend the time to get entertained or just sit and relax.

This way of disconnecting from the work and reconnecting back will help you work more efficiently and helps you produce more output, and this is how you can become productive, and this gives rise to success and satisfaction in life.

Continuously working → gets bored fast → ends up hating your work.

Always try to take breaks in between and do something else other than your work, and this will help you rejuvenate and get back to work.

Productivity secret:

Never work continuously and take frequent breaks.

Try to get disconnected from the work you do and just relax.

45. Creating Vision Chart

"Vision charts help you create transparency for your visions."

Vision charts play a major role in accomplishing your goals, dreams, and passion. Vision charts are simple diagrams, pictures or images which bring your imagination to life. Many people use these vision charts to stay inspired and active at accomplishing their dreams and goals. Vision chart is about designing things you want to acquire in your life, and these charts force your mind to concentrate on things which fulfill your desires, dreams, and goals.

Vision charts play a major role in accomplishing your goals, dreams, and passion. Vision charts are simple diagrams, pictures or images which bring your imagination to life. Many people use these vision charts to stay inspired and active at accomplishing their dreams and goals.

Vision charts have greater influence at accomplishing important things in your life, and they can only be prepared by initiative takers. Dreamers and quitters can never create effective vision charts as their vision is mostly unclear. Therefore you must be able to think clearly to make effective vision charts which will help you accomplish things in time and make you productive.

To make this vision charts, you must undergo two types of personalities. One is dreamers, and another is initiative takers. If you can pursue these two personalities, you could create great vision charts for your life which will inspire you and move forward at accomplishing your desires, dreams, and goals.

First personality: dreamers

This is the first personality you have to pursue. Many people remain as just dreamers as their dreams they dream are impossibilities, or they are of not use in practical life. Therefore dream properly and for right things in life and then only you could become a dreamer or visionary who can make great dreams and visions in mind. The important thing doesn't remain as dreamers, and this will make you hate your life.

Second personality: Initiative takers

You are a dreamer, and you have dreams to accomplish, and you can only accomplish dreams if you pursue initiative taker personality. Don't just stay as a dreamer and do something to accomplish your dreamers. Many people are great visionaries, but if they don't take actions, there is no importance of being a visionary.

Take initiatives to accomplish your dreams. There may be numerous dreams you have to pursue and accomplish, and they may not be enough time to accomplish your every dream. Therefore try to accomplish as many dreams as possible to gain happiness and satisfaction in life. This makes you productive and successful.

Vision charts are the blueprints of your visions in your brain. Everyone has a vision, and we all try to pursue our visions and bring them to live as it gives a lot of satisfaction. Visions may be random or symmetric but accomplishing them gives you satisfaction which you will never get from anything else. This is the super power of vision charts. These vision charts act as catalysts which force you to act fast to accomplish your visions. These are very easy to make and require clear thinking ability to prepare effective vision charts for your life.

It's time to create a vision chart for your vision or dream. What's your vision? Do you want to become a singer? Do you want to become an artist? Or do you want to become an influencer? Whatever your wish or dream or vision may be you are going to get highly inspired from the vision charts and work more efficiently which is a productivity sign.

There is a guy who shared his story of how he got highly benefited from the use of this method. He always dreamt of having a big, beautiful house which captured his attention once. This house is located at a distance of 60km from where he actually lives. He even took a photo of the house which captured his attention and converted it into his vision chart on which he wrote I should own this house in few years and placed the chart in his room and he used to go work after getting inspired by looking at the chart, and this made him work more effectively.

His efficient work brought him several honors and promotions, and in the mean time he shifted to different places, and the vision chart has been moved into store room without his notice. He is growing every day, and he forgot about the house. He has a great life and one day he bought a house with his savings and decided to move into that house.

He moved everything into the house and while arranging things in his new home he came across a box in which his vision chart is found. He took it out and cleared dust over it and just remembered that it is the house he had dreamt of owning and now he is in the house he always dreamt of owning. He fell down on his knees with tears of happiness, and he found great satisfaction that day.

His conscious mind may have forgotten about the house he dreamt of owning but his subconscious mind remembered it very clearly and therefore he owned that house. There is nothing in this world which could give more satisfaction than this.

The real power of vision charts is this. They make you work by getting inspired, and therefore efficient outcome can be expected, and in the mean time, you may forget your dream or goal but some day this vision chart tells you about your accomplishments.

These charts can act as reminders or proofs of your accomplishments. They are very easy to make. They are what you actually want. If you want to own a business, make a vision chart of the business of how it looks in your mind. If you want to own a house, create a map of how that house looks and make it a vision chart. If you want to become a writer, take a print of the cover image of your book and stick it in your room which acts as vision chart and this way of making vision charts helps you become productive and hopeful every day which is full of enthusiasm, energy, and passion.

Productivity secret:

Vision charts help you plan your future at a subconscious level and work more effectively to become or gain what you wished to.

46. Feel free but Be-costlier

"Feel free in the sense have freedom at work. Be-costlier in the sense, stay productive."

This is one more rule which helps you gain more control over work and people. This rule is very important to become productive in life. This chapter concentrates on two different principles which together can create a wonderful mental ability at work which helps you become productive.

The two principles are a) feel-free b) be-costlier. Understanding these two principles gives you clear idea of developing an attitude while working which helps you become efficient at work. The two principles are understood differently and then collectively used to become productive and build a confident mindset and a tough attitude that helps you accomplish more every day.

a. Feel free

This is the most important habit you have to pursue. This is a mental habit which has to be developed. Feel free to work and feel free to think. The important thing you have to learn is, have freedom while accomplishing any task and this will help you perform any task faster and effectively.

There are many people who always feel stressful while working and this will drain your mental and physical energy in you thus making you inefficient at work you do and therefore you will become unproductive. Therefore always have a peaceful mind which can freely think and have a body which always works freely.

This way of working optimize your performance and make you work more efficiently and have success in life. You can work very efficiently by having a whole mindset which is free. Always feel free to become productive in life.

b. Be costlier

This is one more thing you have to understand in life to become productive and satisfied. Becoming costlier is not regarding money, but it's concerning judging you. Stay always more expensive regarding respecting you and have good confidence levels. This way of attitude helps you have control over life and time which is very important to become productive.

Many people feel inferior and sell themselves at very less price. There are several individuals, who are very talented but still gain very less success in their life. This is all because of false assessment they make about themselves. There are many youngsters, who are working at very less pay even though they have talent. All this is because of their wrong judgments about themselves.

There are situations where there is no improvement in salaries and positions of working people, and this is all because of wrong judgments made about them. This is vital to stop judging yourself wrongly to become successful and productive.

An HR of a company has shared her experience about how youngsters compromise with their job and salary, and she said that this compromising behavior is, what making the stay inferior and unsuccessful. She added that they recruit several thousand employees every year into different fields. The most important thing she said is many people who they interview always compromise themselves to work in lower positions and at lower pay which surprised her.

There are also people who are very talented and taken into top positions, but they accept the basic salary without asking for any hike which is more surprising for her at first of her career. She felt that it is not right all. She said that the way the youngsters think and make wrong decisions is very wrong because if they ask for a hike, it may get increased if you are really talented.

This way of compromising happens because of feeling inferiority and lack of confidence. Having talent alone doesn't make you win in life. Along with the talent, you need the confidence to acquire success.

Never make wrong judgments about yourself as your confidence level is based on it. This helps you stay more confident and stay costlier. This, in turn, helps you become more productive and successful.

These two principles as a complex could do more for your success. Always have a free mind which is stated by the first principle and always feel superior which is stated by the second principle and this will help you build a very strong attitude which can be unbroken easily. This will help you grow faster and makes you productive in life.

There is one more thing you have to understand from this chapter. If you don't feel costlier that is superior, you cannot have a free life that is freedom at work in life. Therefore always stay costlier to have a free mind which can make right decisions in time which helps you gain success.

The relation between two principles can be shown by the following equation below:

Be-costlier (feel superior) → Feel free (Gain freedom at work) → more efficient at work → productive life.

Understanding the relation between these two principles is very important to have a peaceful mindset at work, and this will help you concentrate more on work and help you accomplish faster which is a productive sign that helps you gain success.

Start using these two principles to build a strong attitude at the work you do, and these principles can be use to accomplish your dreams or goals or your passion. This method of becoming productive helps you stick to your goals and dreams longer to accomplish them fast

Productivity secret:

Never be available to anyone for free because this world misuses you for their own.

47. Share it for Free Reminders

"Free reminders keep coming when you share what you are working on."

This is one simple way of getting connected to your dream or goal or desire or work in a free and effective manner. This way of connecting helps you to concentrate your mind in accomplishing your dream or desire or goal. Here 'it' in the chapter title refers to your task or goal or desire or dream you have to accomplish. This method helps you to set free reminders and advertise your work to people.

Several successful people and companies use this principle in their marketing campaigns and receive free reminders to accomplish their goals in time. These free reminders tell you or remind you, your goals to accomplish. These reminders act as catalyst or buffer that speed up or balance the working power or interest of you in accomplishing a goal.

Many companies cast their future working projects into public and many movie trailers are released into the public, and several great works are shared with the people before they are actually finished and released. This isn't just a marketing trick, but it shows its influence on workers or performers who are doing it by reminding them again and again what they have to accomplish. These act as reminders which help creators or performers work very faster and complete tasks before deadlines.

These free reminders work great if you can make use of them. These free reminders help you remember your dreams or goals more strongly which helps you concentrate on your work. This high concentration of work helps you accomplish it faster, and this is how free reminders help in productivity development.

This method is the very simple method you can make use of to get free reminders about the goal or work or dream you are pursuing.

The only thing you have to do is share what you are doing with your family or friends or neighbors or someone who is very close to you. When you meet them, they may ask about the progress you are making with your work, and this will help you re-assess the progress you've done as well as it acts as a reminder that tells you to accomplish your work in deadline.

There is a friend of mine who is a freelance writer, and he always completes his work in time and sometimes before the deadlines and when asked how he makes that possible. He answered that he always shares what he is working on with his friends, family and people who are close to him. He also asks those people close to him to query about the progress he makes in his work, and this is how he is able to concentrate on his work to fullest by using these free reminders and make a success.

This method also prevents you from quitting your work. Sometimes you may feel like not doing work, and you decide to quit it, but when people start asking about your progress, you start thinking to finish it again which is necessary and effective to finish accomplishing your goals or dreams.

An amateur author who started writing a book has the problem. He always starts writing with full interest first and gradually he loses interest and quits his work. This happened several times, and he could not even complete a single book. He has several ideas for writing a book, but nothing worked for him.

He started using this method. He shared what he is working on with his friends and used to share what he has written today, and he used to share how much he had completed writing and what is left to write. This way of sharing helped him get reminders about his work and appreciation for what he finished from his friends helps him stay inspired and motivated. This helped him work more efficiently on his work, and he is able to complete writing his books without quitting.

Always make an answer available to the question "what are you doing? Or what are you working on?" and this will help you give a confident and spontaneous answer to people who ask those questions. This will help you spread your accomplishments and works, and this also helps you get back free reminders. This is an important method which helps you gain control over your work and progress.

Productivity secret:

> Share what you are working on with others and ask them to remind what progress you have made every time you meet them. These free reminders actually work well to make you concentrate on your work.

48. Change 'E' Frequently

"Environment plays a major role in productive life as well as personal life."

Changing 'E' is very important to stay active and prevent boredom while working and this will help you become productive at work. The letter 'E' stands for the environment. Changing this environment frequently is done to stay motivated and inspired at work we do. This also helps you prevent boredom. This environment plays a significant role in your work as well as productive life. This environment has complete control over our mind and mood we pursue. Therefore a good environment is very necessary to work more efficiently.

Environment plays a major role in becoming productive at work. Sometimes it has the complete control over the output. Always remember to work in a proper environment to become an efficient worker. Remember to get disconnected from conditions that disturb you or that make you procrastinate.

A fixed environment is always bad, mainly for creative works. This one environment makes you feel bored sitting at one place working for long hours, and therefore you lose interest at work soon and therefore changing environment helps you stay active and work more.

An artist who paints beautiful pictures as well as who illustrate designs has shared his story of how changing environments helps in becoming productive at work. He said that creative work needs freedom to think and this is more possible by keeping our mind to open environment instead of locking it in your working place which is mostly surrounded by walls around you.

A fixed environment in which you work for hours make you feel bored with the work you do, and this will result in unproductivity. You may hate what you are doing even though you are doing what you love and this is all because of creating constraints and barriers in your mind. Therefore environment is one barrier which makes you unproductive. Changing environment has a greater impact on your success.

This human mind can work more efficiently when it is allowed to freely think and act, and this is possible only by making it affected by different environments and make it learn things. This is why changing environments are very necessary to become productive. Working in different environments gives you different thoughts and ideas and when these are together joined to finish your work. The work you accomplish will be the work that inevitably gets you an appraisal.

Always try to work in good environments, and this will help you stay active at the work you do. Always create a work environment that inspires you to work. More about the workspace is explained in initial chapters, and you could read them to create a good working environment.

Change your working environment occasionally when you feel bored with the work you do and this will help you stay more active and concentrate on your work.

Productivity secret:

Always work in a good environment which is free from disturbances to become productive at work.

49. Avoid unnecessary Talks and Meetings

"Attending unnecessary meetings is one of the ways to waste time."

This is one natural habit which is making people lose their valuable time which ultimately results in unproductivity. Many people spend an average of their working time just for additional meetings and talks which make them lose time which could be used to accomplish their works. Socializing with people is important but when it's not necessary it should be avoided to save your time and this time could be used to accomplish important goals and dreams in life.

We all have got one valuable life which is limited in terms of time and therefore it is very important to use this time to excel in life and have satisfaction with living your life. This satisfaction can only be gained by accomplishing your goals in time.

And this accomplishment of goals is possible only by making use of time in a right way without wasting it. These unnecessary meetings and talks are pursued to just pass the time which is really bad. You need to realize the importance of time and never allow time to pass just like by doing nothing which is unproductive. You can never get the time back you have lost. This helps you start concentrating on your productive life and also helps you become successful.

Always avoid unnecessary talks and meetings to have more time in life which could be used for some important things in your life. Go for meetings and talks only when it's necessary to your life. Always have balance in life by having control over time and situations in life.

Even in necessary meetings, you need to speak less and listen more which is a very helpful way of persuasion and learning. This will help you have fewer disturbances in your mind. Speak what is necessary and only when it is necessary. One of my friends used to say that we have got one mouth and two ears are because we need to speak less and listen more. She is very right about it. Always maintain this habit for you to become productive.

Less spoken mouth helps you have a peaceful mind which is a great asset you could have a happy and successful life. Always speak less and listen more to become productive.

There is a man who has a habit of attending unnecessary meetings and chats and this habit in him is because to prevent boredom. He has work to make his habit sometimes caused more harm than good to him. Even during important times, he used to attend unnecessary meetings or chats which made him lose control over success. This made him stay at the position he is, and he didn't grow so much in his career.

When the time has come, he realized it and started avoiding his habit of unnecessary meeting, and soon he became productive as well as satisfied in his life. The only thing that made him very satisfied at his living is proper utilizing of time in very important things in his life.

You can use this principle to make your living wonderful as well as satisfactory. This method is very simple and can be utilized by anyone who wants to become productive as well as who want to accomplish more in life.

Productivity secret:

Never waste time on unnecessary chats and meetings.
You can use this time on something, which makes you productive.

Speak less and listen more to become productive.

50. Bait Works, Use It

"The most part of world runs on hope, bait is one among the types of hope."

Have you ever gone for fishing? Have you at least known how fishing works? Then it's time you should learn more about actual fishing which can be very useful in your practical life. Fishing is done to catch fish but using bait is most important thing to catch fish. The same bait can help you become productive. Many people are already using this baiting system to grow every day. This bait system is a very efficient system which helps you work more with increased hope in you thus making you productive.

This bait system can be used on self or on others to get productive results. This is a simple system, and it states that to accomplish something, reward something.

Bait system → to accomplish a goal, reward or award something

This system can be used in two ways one is bait first, work next, and another is work first, bait next. These two strategies of bait system work great.

The first strategy can be used to influence people to work effectively by giving reward first, and this will inspire them to accomplish more in less time. The second strategy can be used to continue your influence by rewarding them for their outcome from work. These two strategies work great when used correctly in making work more productive. Many companies use these strategies to inspire and motivate the employees and workers of the company to work more efficiently and gain trust and loyalty of employees.

You can use this system for your personal purpose. For example, you will gain something by accomplishing a work which can be explained as you will get something you desire to have in your life by accomplishing a particular task or goal or dream. You can call it bait which you will acquire by performing a task.

For example, a guy who wishes to have a costlier bike thinks of working efficiently in all possible ways to earn money needed to but the costlier bike. The desire that drives him to work effectively has the bike. Bait here is a desire to acquire a bike. Bait could be in different forms, it may be physical or mental.

Physical bait includes all materialistic goods such as a beautiful house, a costlier car; big bank balance, etc. mental bait includes all your feelings, beliefs and thoughts such as social status, fame, love, etc.

The bait, love feeling brings people together and binds them stronger and helps them make better relationships. Bait system is a natural system which can give you effective results.

An owner of a small company used this baiting system and increased the efficiency of employees. He shared his experience of how the bait system helped his company grow faster and also built trust and loyalty of its employees on the enterprise. He started giving away all gifts at first such as surprise tours, promotions, and money vouchers, etc. then he checked for the increased efficiency of workers and the workers. Efficiency is found to be high than before, and along with this, trust and loyalty are built upon the company by employees.

He wants to continue this progress and want to get it into next level that is, he wants to make workers more active at work and bring out more outcomes from their work. Therefore he decided to reward the employees for their every success and this inspired and motivated them to work more efficiently which made the company grow double within a short time. This improved not only employee's productive life but also the conditions of the company, the company culture and people working in it.

You can use two strategies to create a productive environment for your business and also remember to use it at your personal level which helps you concentrate on your work and accomplish it by staying longer with the work. This bait may look unethical, but it is ethical as it supports for good cause and success. Bait system works great if you use it so much and this always gives you productive results.

Productivity secret:

Always use bait system to influence people to work for you effectively.

You can use this system for your own purpose to concentrate more on your work.

PART FOUR

Inspiration Time

The only feeling that drives human mind is an inspiration, and this is how impossibilities become possibilities. Many people get success, but it may not be a great success. There are very fewer people in comparison who actually are successful and happy. Success alone doesn't make you happy and therefore it is not the just one thing you should gain in life. It's human life which is very amazing and wonderful and you have got one. Therefore use it to extreme levels to make your life really satisfying.

Whatever work it may be? How simple or odd it may be? Always get inspired to work, and it always helps you get happiness and satisfaction from the work you do. What inspires you more is what you actually love doing, and this one single trick help you find your passion in life.

There is some magic which runs this whole world and human life is a very amazing thing, and many people had forgotten it. They live like zombies or robots whatever you may call. They don't care about good and evil, and they only care about a luxury life. Money alone became a priority. Human relations got weaker. Success changed its meaning. The bond between human and nature became a broken bond, and we became parasites instead of mutually dependent organisms.

There is greater development in technology. The life of human got better. Transportation facilities have developed. But nothing of this changed human's ill behavior. Nothing of this gave him or her peaceful life. This is all because of illusions ruling this world. The truth is concealed forever. Wisdom is getting lost. This will sum up to a boring lifestyle. People stick more to their mobiles than their family or relations or friends. This is very pity.

Knowledge alone cannot solve your problems every time and always make use of wisdom in life which helps you find good and bad in life. We run like vehicles in getting success, but successes is about living your life to full levels following your heart and mind and always make good which helps you have a peaceful mind.

The real productivity is about living more with fewer worries, and the real success is about getting the success that is permanent which gives you happiness and satisfaction. Always stay wise and active at performing your duties and this one simple rule helps you gain a productive life.

Never postpone things in life because you may not have much time to accomplish hem in the future. Always accomplish things right away, and this will help you gain mental peace and also helps you use the time for your other goals.

Use all the methods practically and find the success in your life and don't just use this guide for reading if you don't want to change because your time is very worthy and you could use it for your goals or dreams. Always stay active and always be a doer.

All the best for a beautiful and productive life…

More Things to Know

There are other things you should be aware to become more productive. These are few more tricks you could make use of to become more productive in life and at work. These are simple yet powerful methods which can be used in your daily life. These skills are random and powerful for having a productive life.

These are the simple yet powerful productivity tricks you can use in your practical life which are as follows:

1. Early to bed and early to rise isn't just a slogan but it's a fact you should make use of in your daily life. Always go to bed soon and wake up early and this helps you stay more active all the day which makes your day amazing and wonderful.
2. Magical morning is the best time for your work. The morning time where there are fewer disturbances is the best time to accomplish more. Therefore use it for achieving your goals or dreams. You can know more about magical morning in the chapters explained above.
3. Learn to meditate every day. It may not give you anything, but it will help you get free from your bad habits.
4. Always accomplish important things first in life. This will help you concentrate on important things in life and helps you save more time.
5. Always accomplish or finish doing the tasks that require very less time and never postpone doing those tasks later thinking them as small tasks.
6. Learn new skills every day, and this will always help you gain active and productive results from work.
7. Learn to worry less because worry causes stress which results in loss of mental peace which in turn results in a lack of concentration power.
8. Never limit yourself because you are one of a kind. Never compare yourself with anyone to live a happy life. Your work is different when you are doing it. You are unique and always try to be unique doing something your way.
9. Know thyself, and this will help you what your strengths and weakness are, and this will help you transform your weakness into strengths which will help you become productive.

10. Follow your heart to find what you love and follow your mind to accomplish what you like and developing this habit helps you win most of the time in life which makes you productive.
11. Productivity isn't just about bringing out more outcomes. It is also about minimizing wastage of any process. For example, you could save your electricity bills by not wasting the unnecessary electricity usage. This will help you save little money which could be used for other purposes.
12. Stress causes you fail at getting started. It also makes you fail at finishing tasks and finally makes you unproductive. Always leave stress to live a happy and peaceful life.

Signing Off Message

Congrats on completing reading this book.

Now you are ready to accomplish more in life. You can start now to achieve your goals, dreams, desires, duties, works and passion projects. Use all methods in your practical life and attain success as well as productive life.

Be a doer, not a speaker. Always accomplish your works and goals and make them express what you are to the world. Read every method carefully and use it for getting productive and success in life.

All the best for having a productive life.

PART FIVE

Summary

Chapter 1

Productivity secret:

Always take healthy foods for proper health.

Always give more importance to your health.

Chapter 2

Productivity secret:

Face one distraction with another distraction

Use very simple techniques or methods to prevent disturbances.

Chapter 3

Productivity secret:

The more you relax mentally, the more mental energy you get.

Chapter 4

Productivity secret:

Find your "Why" at work to become productive.

Finding your, why helps you get inspired.

Chapter 5

Productivity secret:

Develop good habits and these will build your willpower.

Willpower acts as a catalyst that speeds up the performance of any work.

Chapter 6

Productivity secret:

You have very limited life and work more efficiently to accomplish more

Use your energy to peaks to achieve more in your life span.

Chapter 7

Productivity secret:

Never think too much before you do anything.

Just do it approach helps you develop to do it now a habit.

Never fear of anything if you want to be a doer.

Chapter 8

Productivity secret:

Never sit and wait to do nothing

Always pursue some action, and this will help you learn new things in life.

You will become lazy and a procrastinator if you keep waiting for the moment of inspiration.

Chapter 9

Productivity secret:

Always use your full energy to accomplish your goals and dreams.

You have very limited time and unlimited energy.

Chapter 10

Productivity secret:

Self-control can help you have control over time which is very important to become productive.

Self-control can be gained by controlling your mindset.

Chapter 11

Productivity secret:

Willpower helps you accomplish more in less time.

Inspiration acts as a catalyst to grow more will power.

Chapter 12

Productivity secret:

Do every small task that comes in your way.

Do every task immediately which consumes only minutes of time.

Chapter 13

Productivity secret:

Smart cuts are upgraded form of shortcuts.

They are weird ways to which you gain success within very short time.

Chapter 14

Productivity secret:

Continuous use of just do it approach helps you develop to do it now a habit, and this will make your action oriented.

Chapter 15

Productivity secret:

There are no defective plans, and it's the way plan is executed that fails any plan fail, and this happens most of the times.

Effective plans are made by basing one's passion and interest in accomplishing a goal or dream.

Chapter 16

Productivity secret:

A balanced mind is a very rare asset, and you can get it only by experiencing everything in life.

Chapter 17

Productivity secret:

There are several best thinking habits you could develop and some of the best thinking habits to become productive are 9 and are explained above.

Always think independently and rely on yourself.

Think as professional all the way during your work.

Never judge anything at work to be productive.

Chapter 18

Productivity secret:

Learn a skill every day related to your work

Learn a new skill every day which may be you are passionate about.

Learn to evaluate you to find development

Chapter 19

Productivity secret:

Always minimize the number of steps in a process.

Take one big step or several steps to improve or reinvent a process or pathway.

Chapter 20

Productivity secret:

To make accuracy and speed, stay together while working or performing a task, love the work you do or grow interested in work you do.

You can grow your interest in work by learning new skills and tricks which help you accomplish your work faster and in an effective way.

Chapter 21

Productivity secret:

Carry a log book and a pen whenever you travel because thoughts flow just like your journey.

Listen to an audio book or podcast while traveling.

Chapter 22

Productivity secret:

The best working environment is a very necessary aspect to become productive.

Clean workspace helps you have a peaceful mind.

Chapter 23

Productivity secret:

Action posters help you remember your goals and dreams.

Design action posters in a beautiful way.

Chapter 24

Productivity secret:

Advance plans help you stay prepared for tomorrow

Advance planning helps you build a secure future.

Chapter 25

Productivity secret:

Learn to be an introvert at work because they are very less distracted at work.

Chapter 26

Productivity secret:

Break a bigger task into several small parts until it feels very easy to start and finish.

Chapter 27

Productivity secret:

Filtering system for tasks or goals or dreams helps you concentrate more on important things.

Chapter 28

Productivity secret:

There are several barriers which make to a procrastinator. Try avoiding those barriers.

Chapter 29

Productivity secret:

Never worry about results which surely occur at the end of any process. This will help you become stress-free at work.

Chapter 30

Productivity secret:

Try to take breaks when you get bored, and this recharges your mind and body.

Chapter 31

Productivity secret:

Never perform any task in a hurry because the result will be mostly a failure.

Chapter 32

Productivity secret:

Comparing now and then helps you find progress and helps you become more productive.

Now and later charts help you frame a plan to become something in future.

Chapter 33

Productivity secret:

Only work don't fulfill your living, and there are several things you need to experience in your life to be called as a productive person.

Spend time for something which will help you grow interest, in life.

Chapter 34

Productivity secret:

Creative works need more mental energy and less physical energy. Formal or casual works need high physical energy and less mental energy.

Chapter 35

Productivity secret:

Morning time has fewer disturbances and is the perfect time for performing very important things in life.

Chapter 36

Productivity secret:

Discipline helps you stay in control and this, in turn, helps you have control over the external world.

Chapter 37

Productivity secret:

When size matters, think small. Always make use of small lists to plan better and accomplish better.

Chapter 38

Productivity secret:

Learn from others and learn best methods for work to easily become productive and successful.

Chapter 39

Productivity secret:

It's better to create your own method, and the easiest way would transform a perfect method to work for you.

Chapter 40

Productivity secret:

Over-thinking is one of the biggest mental barriers which make people become procrastinators.

Think till your brain produce positive thoughts and when it starts producing negative thoughts. Stop thinking and start working

Chapter 41

Productivity secret:

Fear is one biggest barrier which destroys your productive life.

To prevent fear, you need to stop worrying about it and start working.

Chapter 42

Productivity secret:

Addictions make you fail at concentrating at work.

Addictions can be prevented or cured by taking small steps to change you.

Chapter 43

Productivity secret:

Do the work you love to become productive and successful.

Love the work you do to find passion in your work and love it.

Chapter 44

Productivity secret:

Never work continuously and take frequent breaks.

Try to get disconnected from the work you do and just relax.

Chapter 45

Productivity secret:

Vision charts help you plan your future at a subconscious level and work more effectively to become or gain what you wished to.

Chapter 46

Productivity secret:

Never be available to anyone for free because this world mis uses you for their own.

Chapter 47

Productivity secret:

Share what you are working on with others and ask them to remind what progress you have made every time you meet them. These free reminders really work well to make you concentrate on your work.

Chapter 48

Productivity secret:

Always work in a good environment which is free from disturbances to become productive at work.

Chapter 49

Productivity secret:

Never waste time on unnecessary chats and meetings. You can use this time on something, which makes you productive.

Speak less and listen more to become productive.

Chapter 50

Productivity secret:

Always use bait system to influence people to work for you effectively.

You can use this system for your own purpose to concentrate more on your work.

Productivity Quotes you Could use in Your Life

Time is a beautiful illusion created by a human which is controlling human.

Time is a modern scale for measuring success and failure in life.

Time becomes your best friend when this becomes a principle of work in your life that is a passion first, everything next.

Nothing is impossible unless you start doing it.

Starting is the difficult thing, and then everything goes better.

This is productivity rule: Stop talking and start doing.

Work on the process and forget about the results and this is the simple rule for accomplishing any work.

They are called as poor not the one who has no money but the one who always say they have no time for big things in life.

Take risks, and this will help you accomplish more in life.

Time and light have one thing in common. You can see the light but can never catch it, and you can see time moving on, but you can never catch it.

Calm nature and peaceful human have one thing in common. They both seem to be doing nothing but something will be happening.

Do amazing things today not tomorrow.

Learning is a habit which boosts your productivity life.

Never allow your failures to influence your productive life.

Work with a deep purpose rather than a deep need to excel in life and at work.

Hard work alone can build a beautiful castle of success.

Productivity is about making things better in life every day.

Pay attention and gain results from work.

Procrastinators wait for the moment of inspiration and keep waiting for it and end up not finding it anyway.

Do it today and tomorrow may be just an illusion.

Over thinking will not help you accomplish things in life.

Become a doer, not a procrastinator.

Failures knock you down again and again in life and let your failure know that you are getting built to face the biggest fight of life.

How cool it would be if you get addicted to your watch just like you stick or addict to some other technology gadgets such as mobiles and computers.

Tomorrow is an illusion if you can't find the importance of today in your life.

Your proper actions make motions more autonomous.

Make mistakes and learn because who make mistakes and never learn become inferiors and who make mistakes and learn become superiors.

If it's "not now" it may be "never'.

It's happening, so don't sit and stare idly.

Effective productivity is about doing right things in a right way and right away.

If you love your work, do it. If you hate your work, love it.

Think twice before you do and try accomplishing as many times as possible before you quit.

Make all necessary tools available to become productive by accomplishing work

Take time to think and accomplish and be patient for the results.

Better to be productive than being busy.

Follow your heart to find your passion and follow your mind to pursue your passion.

If you can control time, then you can control everything in your life.

Productivity is not about doing more, but it's about doing least with betterment.

Be cautious with overtime, it makes you unproductive.

Make fun working on what you love, and this is a simple principle for happy work life.

Work with a purpose not with a need.

Allow your thoughts to flow in your brain and then into your actions.

Don't judge your work; anyhow you have to accomplish it.

Work on your passion or find your passion or make what you are working on your passion.

Success is very simple regarding life; it is just "live it high."

Find time to have peace because it is the fuel that charges your mind and body.

Productivity is about doing something you never did to accomplish something you never had.

Actions speak more loudly than your words, keep acting.

The tight deadlines help you accomplish more in less time.

Time is very limited, and your energy is unlimited. Learn to balance them to become productive.

Life is a journey. Make your journey exciting by accomplishing great every day.

Don't over think, just do it.

Amazing things are happening today and how about making one.

Few run behind time, and they are successful but not happy and few run against time and they are a failure and few others run along with the time and they are successful and happy.

There are three hands on a clock or watch. Seconds hand says start fast because there no much time left. Minutes hand means think and act moderately. Hours hand says have the patience to get success.

PART SIX

Assessment Resources

You can find these free resources available to only the readers of this book. These are high-value resources which are helpful in making your life more productive. The links are placed in the final part of this book. Go to the productivity guide website for more tricks and tips to on productivity.

Podcast Resources

You can find podcasts on various topics online. To find them you can go and search author name + podcast on Google or find those on iTunes by searching author name, and also you can find them on sound cloud. Find audio resources on the website. They are free to listen and start using them in your life.

PART SEVEN

Other Works by Author

Quotes of wisdom-1 – self-help

Quotes of wisdom-2 – self-help

The rhythm of life – self-help

The last tree of wishes – short story

59 powerful productivity secrets – self-help

Productivity for students – self-help

Important Links:

Productivity Project Website:

www.productivityguide.net

Author Website:

www.manikantabelde.com

www.manikantabelde.net

Blog:

www.manikantabelde.wordpress.com

www.manimagicworld.blogspot.com

Facebook:

www.facebook.com/manikantabelde

Twitter:

www.twitter.com/manikantabelde

Feedback @

Email: admin@manikantabelde.com

About Author

www.manikantabelde.com/about/

Project productivity helps you become productive by getting inspired in a natural way.

This is the first ever guide on the planet which helps you grow productivity lifestyle in a natural way

Know more at:

www.productivityguide.net

www.ingramcontent.com/pod-product-compliance
Lightning Source LLC
Chambersburg PA
CBHW020642220526
45464CB00001B/258